Reteach

Author

Dr Fong Ho Kheong

 Marshall Cavendish
Education

U.S. Distributor

**Houghton
Mifflin
Harcourt**

© 2015 Marshall Cavendish Education Private Limited

Published by Marshall Cavendish Education
An imprint of Marshall Cavendish Education Private Limited
Times Centre, 1 New Industrial Road, Singapore 536196
Customer Service Hotline: (65) 6213 9444
U.S. Office Tel: (1-914) 332 8888 Fax: (1-914) 332 8882
E-mail: tmesales@mceducation.com
Website: www.mceducation.com

Distributed by
Houghton Mifflin Harcourt
222 Berkeley Street
Boston, MA 02116
Tel: 617-351-5000
Website: www.hmheducation.com/mathinfocus

First published 2015

Math in Focus® Reteach 1A
ISBN 978-0-544-19247-8

Printed in Singapore

1 2 3 4 5 6 7 8   1401   20 19 18 17 16 15
4500463652   A B C D E

Contents

Subtraction Facts to 10

Shapes and Patterns

CHAPTER 6 Ordinal Numbers and Position

CHAPTER 7 Numbers to 20

CHAPTER 8 Addition and Subtraction Facts to 20

Length

Introducing

Math in Focus®

Reteach

Reteach 1A and *1B*, written to complement *Math in Focus®: Singapore Math® by Marshall Cavendish* Grade 1, offer a second opportunity to practice skills and concepts at the entry level. Key vocabulary terms are explained in context, complemented by sample problems with clearly worked solutions.

Not all children are able to master a new concept or skill after the first practice. A second opportunity to practice at the same level before moving on can be key to long-term success.

Monitor students' levels of understanding during daily instruction and as they work on Practice exercises. Provide *Reteach* worksheets for extra support to students who would benefit from further practice at a basic level.

 Numbers to 10

Worksheet 1   Counting to 10

Count.

Match the ⬡ **groups to the** △ **groups.**

1.

     •─────────────────────•

   •   •

     •   •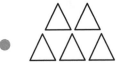

     •   •

Count.
Write the number.

 **Example**

numbers

1 2 3 4 5
6 7 8 9 10

There are ____5____  .

2.

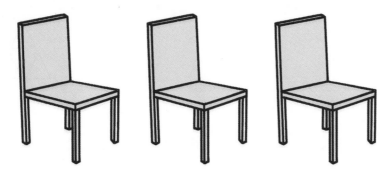

There are _____ .

3.

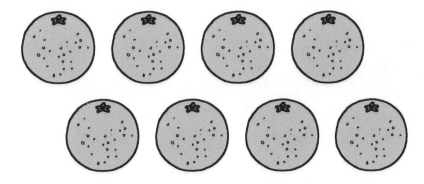

There are _____  .

4.

There are _____ 🐝 .

5.

There are _____ .

6.

There is _____ 🛏.

There are _____ 🪑.

There are _____ 🍽.

There are _____ ☕.

Count.
Write the number.

─── **Example** ───

7.

8. Draw 🌙 in the ☐☐☐☐☐ to show the number.

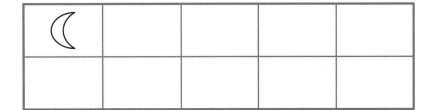

9. Draw △ in the ☐☐☐☐☐ to show the number.

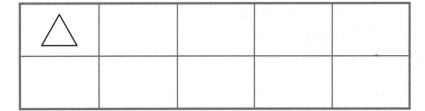

Check (✓) the correct box.

10. Which plate has 0 ?

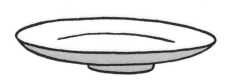

11. Which nest has zero ?

● **Match the numbers to the words.**

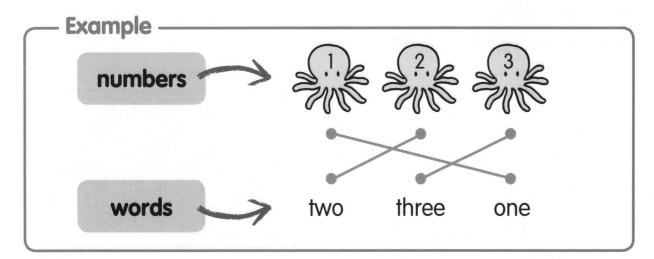

Example

numbers ➜

words ➜   two   three   one

12.

●

four   nine   six

13.

eight   zero   five   ten

14.

●

five   three   seven   four

Count.
Fill in the blanks.
Use the words in the box.

five	nine
three	eight
ten	six
seven	two

--- **Example** ---

 bananas _____*five*_____

15. apples _____

16. lemons _____

17. oranges _____

18. strawberries _____

19. cherries _____

Worksheet 2   Comparing Numbers

Match.
Compare.
Fill in the blanks with *more*, *fewer*, or *same*.

Example

There are _____*more*_____ cups than saucers.
There are _____*fewer*_____ saucers than cups.

1.

There are _____ cups than saucers.

2.

The number of cups and the number of saucers are the _____.

3.

There are _____ cups than saucers.

Fill in the blanks with *more* or *fewer*.

4.

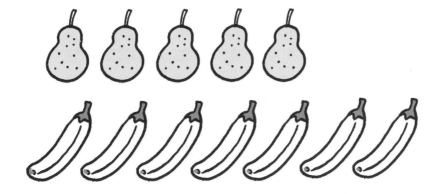

There are _____ pears than bananas.

There are _____ bananas than pears.

5.

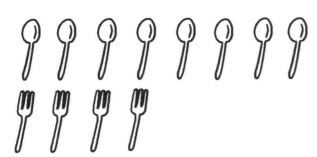

There are _____ spoons than forks.

There are _____ forks than spoons.

Write the numbers in the boxes.

Color the ⬚⬚⬚⬚⬚ that has **more**.

Example

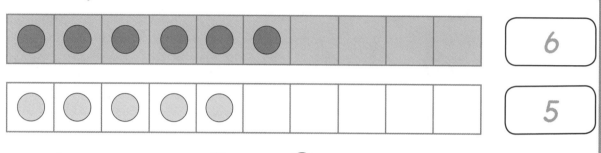

There are **more** ⬤ than ◯.

6.

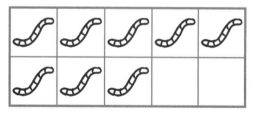

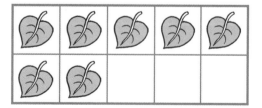

7.

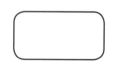

● **Write the numbers in the boxes.**

Color the ☐☐☐☐☐ **that has <u>fewer</u>.**

> **Example**
>
> | 🌻 | 🌻 | 🌻 | 🌻 | 🌻 | | | | | |
>
> 5
>
> | 🌸 | 🌸 | 🌸 | | | | | | | |
>
> 3
>
> There are **fewer**  than 🌻.

8.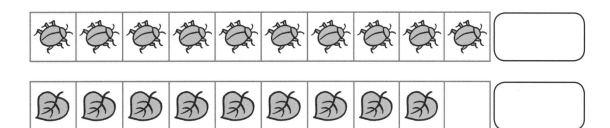

9.

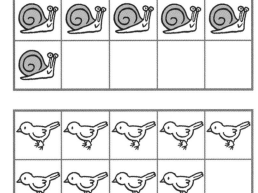

Fill in the blanks with numbers.

Example

Which number is greater?
Which number is less?

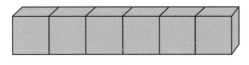

6

4

There are 6  and 4 ☐.

There are more ☐ than ☐.

___6___ is **greater than** ___4___.

There are fewer ☐ than ■.

___4___ is **less than** ___6___.

---

10. Which number is less?

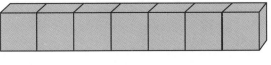

7

9

_____ is less than _____.

11. Which number is greater?

8

4

_____ is greater than _____.

12. Which number is greater?

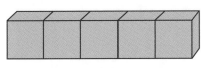

5

6

_____ is greater than _____.

Fill in the blanks with *hens, ducks,* or *goats*.

13.

The number of _____ is the same as the

number of _____.

14. Write a number that is greater than 7. _____

15. Write a number that is less than 4. _____

Worksheet 3   Making Number Patterns

Fill in the blanks.

> **Example**
>
> 1, ___2___, ___3___, 4, 5

1.   1, 2, _____, _____, 5

2.   _____, 2, _____, 4, 5

3.   6, 7, _____, _____, 10

4.   _____, 7, _____, 9, 10

5.   _____, 7, 8, _____, _____

Look for a pattern.

Example

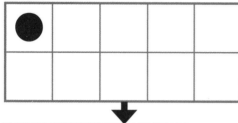

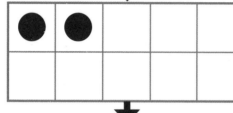

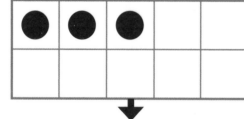

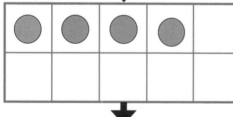

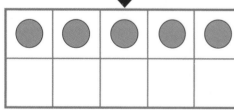

Continue the pattern.

pattern

1, 2, 3, 4, 5

Look for a pattern.
Continue the pattern.

6.

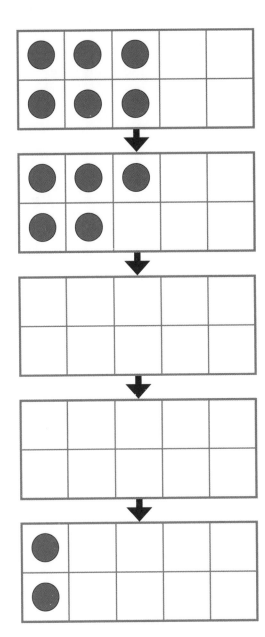

Fill in these ten frames to complete the pattern.

7. Color the ☐ to show 1 less than 6.

6 ☐☐☐☐☐☐

8. Draw ☐ to show 1 more than 5.

5 ☐☐☐☐☐

9. Draw the ☐ in the correct order to make a pattern.

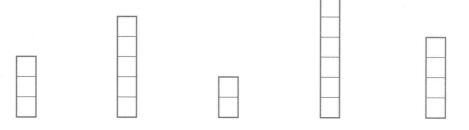

2 Number Bonds

Worksheet 1 Making Number Bonds

Count the number of .

Write the number in the ⬭.

1.   ▭▭▭   ⬭

2.   ▭▭   ⬭

Count the number of ⬜.

Write the numbers in the ⬭.

┌─ **Example** ──────────────────────────────┐
│
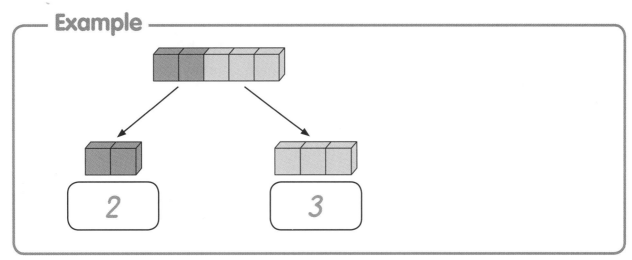

       2   3
│
└──┘

3.

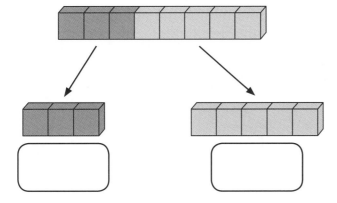

What numbers make 4?

Write the numbers in the ◯.

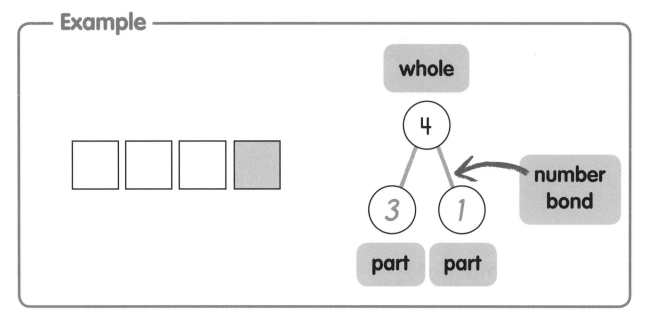

— Example —

whole

4

3   1   ← number bond

part   part

4.

   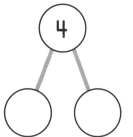

5.

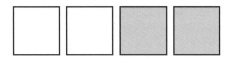   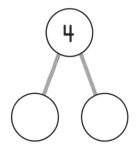

Color the ☐ to show two parts.
Then write the numbers in the ◯.

Example

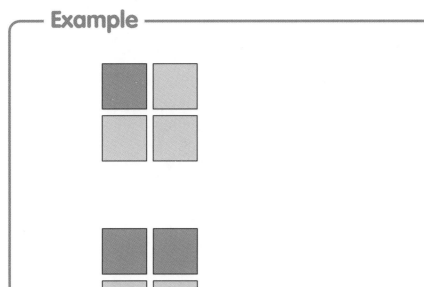

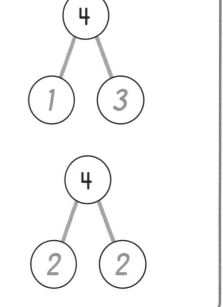

6.

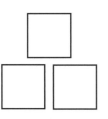

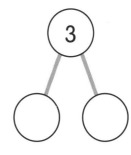

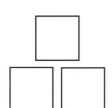

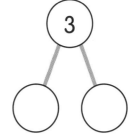

7.

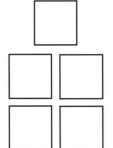
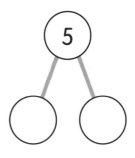

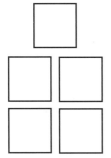
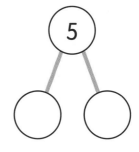

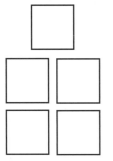
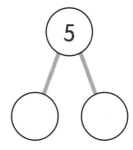

Worksheet 2 Making Number Bonds

What are the parts that make the whole?
Circle the things to show the numbers in the number bonds.

Example

1.

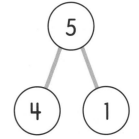

2.

3.

Name: _____   **Date:** _____

Count.
Fill in the blanks.

4.

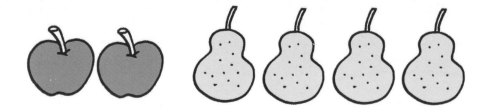

There are _____ apples.

There are _____ pears.

There are _____ pieces of fruit in all.

5.

There is _____ black butterfly.

There are _____ white butterflies.

There are _____ butterflies in all.

6.

There are _____ boys.

There are _____ girls.

There are _____ children in all.

Worksheet 3   Making Number Bonds

Match to make 6.
Complete the number bonds.

1.

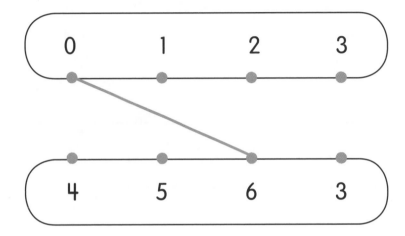

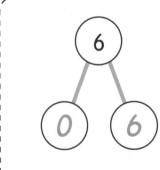
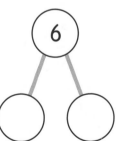
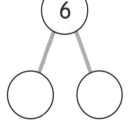

Match to make 10.
Complete the number bonds.

2.

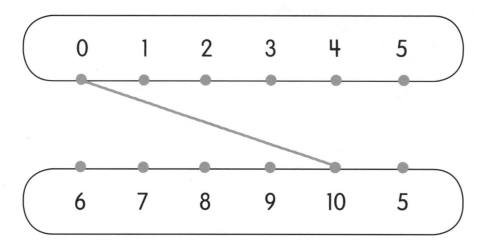

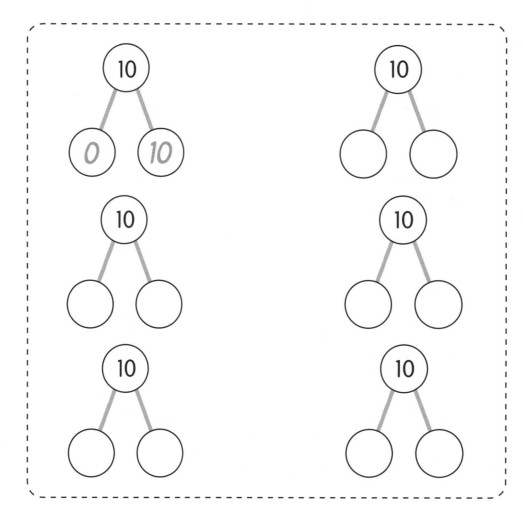

Addition Facts to 10

Worksheet 1   Ways to Add

Count.
Write the number.

1.

2.

What comes next?
Fill in the blanks.

3.   1, 2, 3, 4, _____, _____

4.   6, 7, 8, _____, _____

Add.
Count on from the greater number.

```
┌─ Example ────────────────────────────────────────────────┐
```

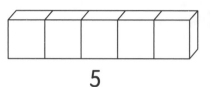

5   3

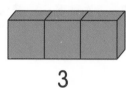

5, __*6*__, __*7*__, __*8*__

5 + 3 = __*8*__

To **add** means to put together.

5 + 3 = 8 is an addition sentence. + is read as **plus**. It means add. = means **equal to**.

5.

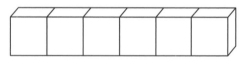 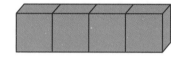

6   4

6, _____, _____, _____, _____

6 + 4 = _____

6.

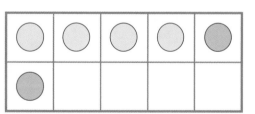

_____, _____, _____

4 + 2 = _____

7.

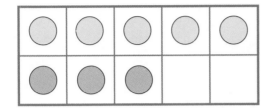

_____, _____, _____, _____

5 + 3 = _____

Count on to add.
Fill in the blanks.

┌─ **Example** ──────────────────────────────────────┐

What is 2 **more than** 4?

____2____ is **added on to** ____4____.

4, ____5____, ____6____

____6____ is 2 more than 4.

| **More than**
| means **added**
| **on to**.

└──┘

8. What is 3 more than 7?

_____ is added on to _____.

7, _____, _____, _____

_____ is 3 more than 7.

9. What is 4 more than 6?

6, _____, _____, _____, _____

_____ is 4 more than 6.

Look at the cubes.
Count on from the greater number.

10.

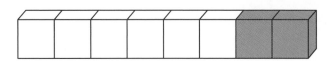

2 more than 6 is _____.

_____ is 2 more than 6.

11.

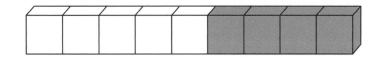

4 more than 5 is _____.

_____ is 4 more than 5.

12.

3 more than 5 is _____.

_____ is 3 more than 5.

13.

4 more than 6 is _____.

_____ is 4 more than 6.

Count on to add.
Then fill in the blanks.
Use the counting tape to help you.

Example

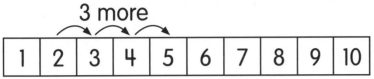

3 more

| 1 | 2 | 3 | 4 | 5 | 6 | 7 | 8 | 9 | 10 |

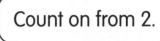

Count on from 2.

____5____ is 3 more than 2.

A **counting tape** can help you to count on.

14.

| 1 | 2 | 3 | 4 | 5 | 6 | 7 | 8 | 9 | 10 |

_____ is 2 more than 6.

15.

| 1 | 2 | 3 | 4 | 5 | 6 | 7 | 8 | 9 | 10 |

_____ is 3 more than 7.

16.

1	2	3	4	5	6	7	8	9	10

Jen counted 2 more than a number.
She stopped at 3.
At what number did she start counting?

17.

1	2	3	4	5	6	7	8	9	10

Ben counted 3 more than a number.
He stopped at 10.
At what number did he start counting?

Worksheet 2   Ways to Add

Complete the number bonds.

1.

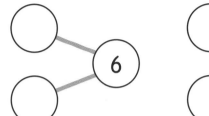

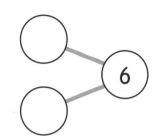

Complete the number bonds.
Then fill in the blanks.

Example

_____5_____ + _____3_____ = _____8_____

2.

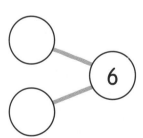

_____ + _____ = _____

3.

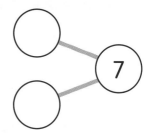

_____ + _____ = _____

4.

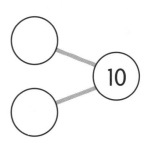

_____ + _____ = _____

5.

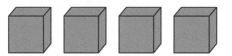

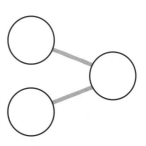

_____ + _____ = _____

6.

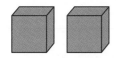

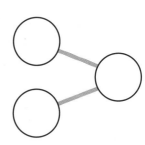

_____ + _____ = _____

Complete the number bonds in two ways.

Example

How many children are there in all?

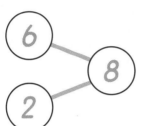

_6_ + _2_ = _8_   _2_ + _6_ = _8_

7. How many flowers are there in all?

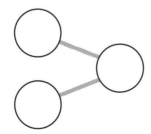

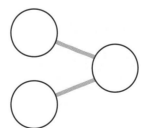

_____ + _____ = _____   _____ + _____ = _____

Use two colors. Color the  to show an addition sentence in two ways.

Fill in the blanks.

Example

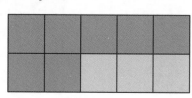 

__7__ + __3__ = __10__   __3__ + __7__ = __10__

8.

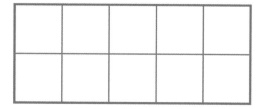 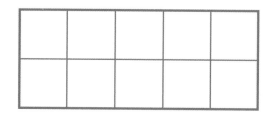

_____ + _____ = _____   _____ + _____ = _____

Worksheet 3   Making Addition Stories

Use the pictures to make addition stories.
Use number bonds to help you.

Example

There are ____4____  .

There are ____3____ .

____4____ + ____3____ = ____7____

There are ____7____ 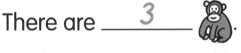 and  in all.

4
3
7

1.

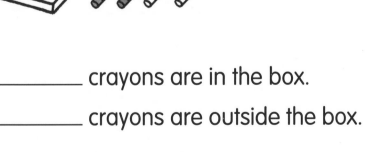

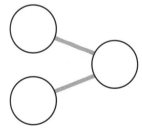

_____ crayons are in the box.

_____ crayons are outside the box.

_____ + _____ = _____

There are _____ crayons in all.

2.

There are _____ white birds.

There are _____ gray birds.

_____ + _____ = _____

There are _____ birds in all.

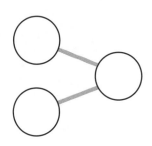

3.

Alice has _____ white cats.

She has _____ spotted cats.

Alice has _____ cats in all.

4.

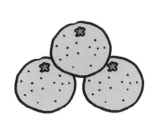
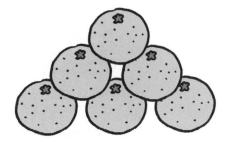

Janice   Penny

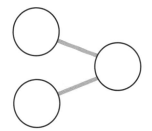

Janice buys _____ grapefruits.

Penny buys _____ grapefruits.

Janice and Penny buy _____ grapefruits in all.

5.

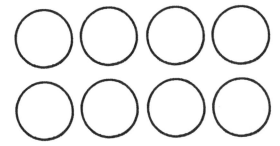

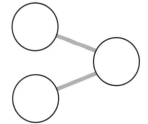

José has _____ white balls.

He also has _____ black balls.

José has _____ balls in all.

6.

Plate A   Plate B

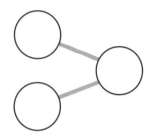

Mary has _____ muffins on Plate A.

She has _____ muffins on Plate B.

Mary has _____ muffins in all.

7.

Terence has _____ toy cars.

He has _____ toy trains.

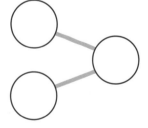

Terence has _____ toys in all.

Worksheet 4 Real-World Problems: Addition

Solve.
Fill in the blanks. Use number bonds to help you.

1.

There are 5 math books on the table.
There are 3 English books on the table.
How many books are there in all?

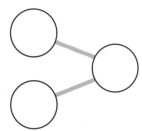

_____ + _____ = _____

There are _____ books in all.

2.

Jenny has 3 coins.
Larry gives her 6 coins.
How many coins does Jenny have now?

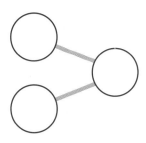

_____ + _____ = _____

Jenny has _____ coins now.

3.

There are 7 colored pencils in a box.
Will puts 2 more pencils in the box.
How many pencils are there in the box
after Will is done?

_____ ◯ _____ = _____

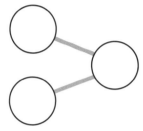

There are _____ pencils in the box.

4.

Plate A   Plate B

There are 9 strawberries on Plate A.
There are no strawberries on Plate B.
How many strawberries are there in all?

_____ + _____ = _____

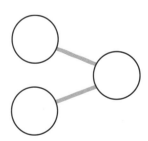

There are _____ strawberries in all.

CHAPTER 4 Subtraction Facts to 10

Worksheet 1   Ways to Subtract

Fill in the blanks.

1.   4, 5, _____, _____, 8

2.   3, 4, _____, _____, _____, 8

3.   8, 7, _____, _____, _____

4.   5, 4, _____, _____, _____, _____

Fill in the blanks.

5.

_____ is 1 less than 8.

6.

1 less than 9 is _____.

Cross out to subtract.
Then complete the subtraction sentence.

┌─ **Example** ───┐

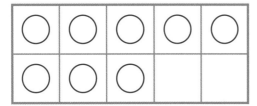

To subtract means to
take away.
Crossing out 2 ◯ means
to take away 2 ◯.

5 − 2 = ___*3*___

5 − 2 = 3 is a
subtraction sentence.
− is read as **minus**.
It means **subtract**.

└──┘

7.

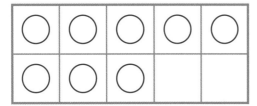

8 − 2 = _____

8.

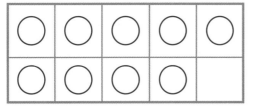

9 − 5 = _____

Complete the subtraction sentences.

9.

7 – _____ = _____

10.

9 – _____ = _____

11.

6 – _____ = _____

12.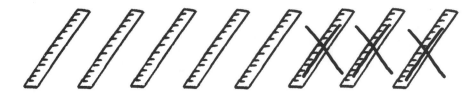

8 – _____ = _____

Cross out to subtract.
Then complete the subtraction sentence.

Example

What is 3 less than 5?

Less than means taken away from.
3 is taken away from 5.

5 − 3 = ___2___

___2___ is 3 less than 5.

13.

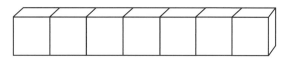

What is 2 less than 7?

7 − 2 = _____

_____ is 2 less than 7.

14.

What is 3 less than 8?

8 − _____ = _____

_____ is 3 less than 8.

15.

What is 6 less than 10?

10 − _____ = _____

_____ is 6 less than 10.

Name: _____ **Date:** _____

● **Subtract.**
Count on from the number that is less.
Fill in the blanks.

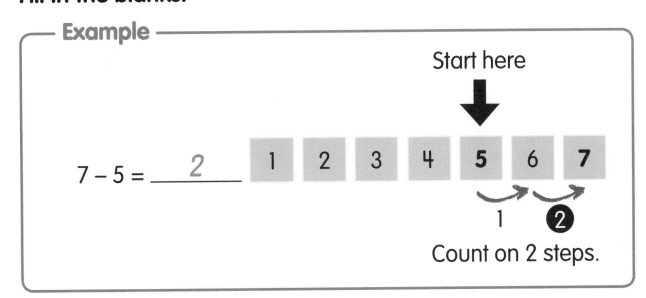

Example

$7 - 5 =$ ___2___

Start here

| 1 | 2 | 3 | 4 | **5** | 6 | **7** |

1 ②

Count on 2 steps.

● **16.** $9 - 6 =$ _____

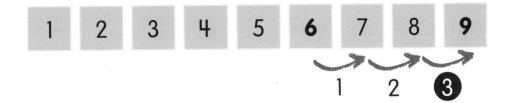

| 1 | 2 | 3 | 4 | 5 | **6** | 7 | 8 | **9** |

1   2   ③

Count on _____ steps.

17. $8 - 4 =$ _____

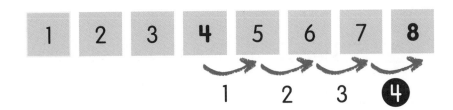

| 1 | 2 | 3 | **4** | 5 | 6 | 7 | **8** |

1   2   3   ④

●

Count on _____ steps.

18.   10 – 5 = _____

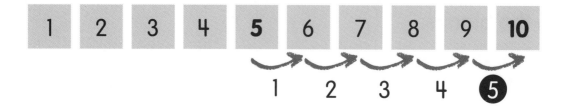

Count on _____ steps.

19.   7 – 2 = _____

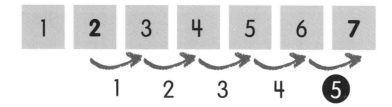

Count on _____ steps.

20.   10 – 7 = _____

Count on _____ steps.

Subtract.
Count back from the greater number.
Fill in the blanks.

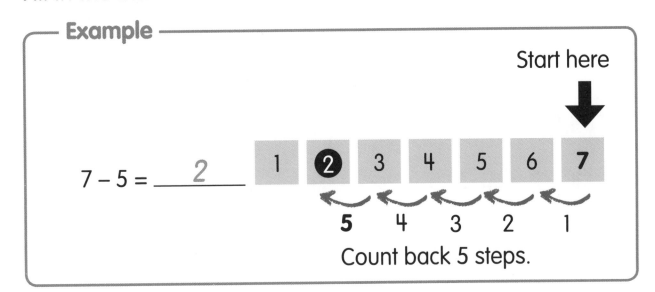

Example

Start here

$7 - 5 =$ ___2___

1 ② 3 4 5 6 **7**

5 4 3 2 1

Count back 5 steps.

21. $8 - 6 =$ _____

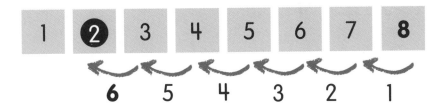

1 ② 3 4 5 6 7 **8**

6 5 4 3 2 1

Count back _____ steps.

22. 6 – 1 = _____

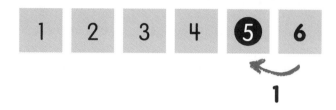

Count back _____ step.

23. 10 – 3 = _____

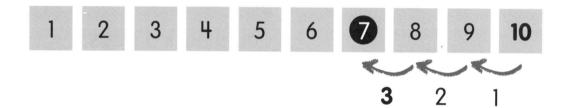

Count back _____ steps.

24. 4 – 4 = _____

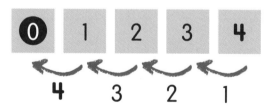

Count back _____ steps.

Worksheet 2   Ways to Subtract

Complete the number bond.

1.

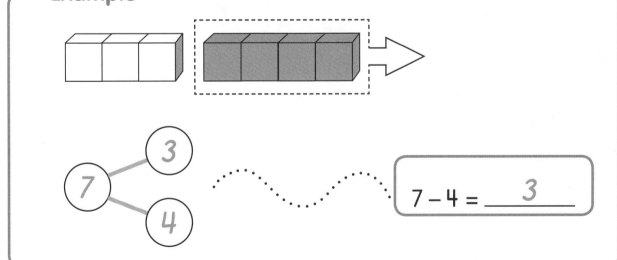

Fill in the number bonds.
Then complete the subtraction sentences.

┌─ **Example** ─────────────────────────────────┐

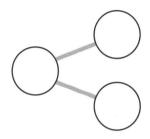

7 – 4 = ____3____

└──┘

2.

4 − 1 = _____

3.

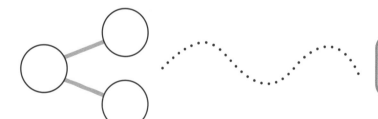

9 − 4 = _____

4.

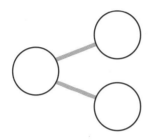

$$\underline{\hspace{2cm}} - \underline{\hspace{2cm}} = \underline{\hspace{2cm}}$$

5.

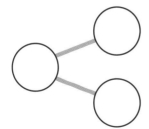

$$\underline{\hspace{2cm}} - \underline{\hspace{2cm}} = \underline{\hspace{2cm}}$$

6.

_____ – _____ = _____

7.

_____ – _____ = _____

Worksheet 3   Making Subtraction Stories

Look at the pictures.
Make subtraction stories.
Write subtraction sentences for each story.

— Example —

There are ___7___ insects.

There are ___2___ butterflies.

$7 - 2 = 5$

There are ___5___ bees.

1.

There are _____ flowers.

There are _____ roses.

There are _____ sunflowers.

2.

There are _____ pieces of fruit.

There are _____ apples.

There are _____ grapefruits.

3.

Carlos has _____ dogs.

There are _____ white dogs.

There are _____ black dogs.

4.

There are _____ animals.

There are _____ chickens.

There are _____ ducks.

5.

Patsy has _____ kittens.

She sold _____ kittens.

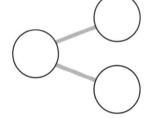

| | ◯ | | ◯ | |

Patsy has _____ kittens left.

Worksheet 4   Real-World Problems: Subtraction

Fill in the number bonds.
Solve.

1.

There are 7 books in a school bag.
3 of the books are math books.
The rest are English books.
How many English books are there?

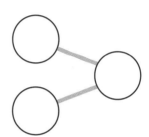

_____ − _____ = _____

There are _____ English books.

2.

There are 8 ladybugs.
4 ladybugs are flying away.
How many ladybugs are left?

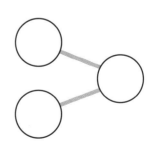

_____ − _____ = _____

There are _____ ladybugs left.

© Marshall Cavendish International (Singapore) Private Limited.

3.

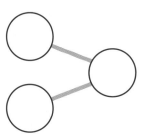

Shirley has 10 coins.
She gives Alicia 4 coins.
How many coins does Shirley have left?

_____ – _____ = _____

Shirley has _____ coins left.

4.

Christine has 7 towels.
2 towels are wet.
How many dry towels does Christine have?

_____ – _____ = _____

Christine has _____ dry towels.

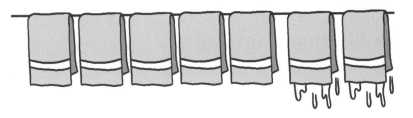

Worksheet 5 Making Fact Families

Write a fact family for each picture.

Example

This is a **fact family**. 3 and 6 are parts. 9 is a whole.

Remember to use the same parts and whole.

__3__ + __6__ = __9__
__6__ + __3__ = __9__
__9__ − __6__ = __3__
__9__ − __3__ = __6__

1.

____ + ____ = ____
____ + ____ = ____
____ − ____ = ____
____ − ____ = ____

2.

____ + ____ = ____
____ + ____ = ____
____ − ____ = ____
____ − ____ = ____

Write a fact family for each number bond.

Example

part **3**

9 whole

part **6**

$$\underline{\quad 3 \quad} + \underline{\quad 6 \quad} = \underline{\quad 9 \quad}$$
$$\underline{\quad 6 \quad} + \underline{\quad 3 \quad} = \underline{\quad 9 \quad}$$
$$\underline{\quad 9 \quad} - \underline{\quad 6 \quad} = \underline{\quad 3 \quad}$$
$$\underline{\quad 9 \quad} - \underline{\quad 3 \quad} = \underline{\quad 6 \quad}$$

3.

3

10

7

$$\underline{\qquad} + \underline{\qquad} = \underline{\qquad}$$
$$\underline{\qquad} + \underline{\qquad} = \underline{\qquad}$$
$$\underline{\qquad} - \underline{\qquad} = \underline{\qquad}$$
$$\underline{\qquad} - \underline{\qquad} = \underline{\qquad}$$

4.

5

8

3

$$\underline{\qquad} + \underline{\qquad} = \underline{\qquad}$$
$$\underline{\qquad} + \underline{\qquad} = \underline{\qquad}$$
$$\underline{\qquad} - \underline{\qquad} = \underline{\qquad}$$
$$\underline{\qquad} - \underline{\qquad} = \underline{\qquad}$$

● **Use the numbers to make a fact family.**

5.
     _____ + _____ = _____

     _____ + _____ = _____

     _____ − _____ = _____

     _____ − _____ = _____

6.
     _____ + _____ = _____

     _____ + _____ = _____

     _____ − _____ = _____

     _____ − _____ = _____

● **Find the missing number.**
Use the numbers to make a fact family.

7.   3, 4, [   ]

     _____ + _____ = _____

     _____ + _____ = _____

     _____ − _____ = _____

     _____ − _____ = _____

There is more than one correct answer.

Solve.
Use related facts to help you.

8. Sarah has some marbles.
She gives away 6 marbles.
She has 2 marbles left.
How many marbles did Sarah have at first?

$$\boxed{} - 6 = 2$$

$6 + 2 = \boxed{}$ is the related addition fact.

Sarah had _____ marbles at first.

9. Jeffrey has 5 erasers.
Gina gives Jeffrey some erasers.
Jeffrey now has 9 erasers.
How many erasers did Gina give Jeffrey?

$5 + \boxed{} = 9$

$9 - 5 = \boxed{}$ is the related subtraction sentence.

Gina gave Jeffrey _____ erasers.

Find the missing numbers.
Use related facts to fill in the blanks.

Example

$3 +$ __4__ $= 7$

__7__ $-$ __3__ $=$ __4__

What should I add to 3 to make 7?

1. Count on

   3, 4, 5, 6, 7
      1 2 3 4

2. Number bonds

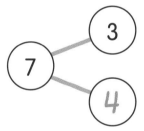

10. $4 +$ _____ $= 9$

_____ $-$ _____ $=$ _____

11. _____ $+ 2 = 6$

_____ $-$ _____ $=$ _____

Name: ______________________ Date: ______________

12. ________ + 3 = 3

________ − ________ = ________

13. 8 − ________ = 3

________ + ________ = ________

14. 9 − ________ = 7

________ + ________ = ________

15. ________ − 4 = 5

________ + ________ = ________

16. ________ − 3 = 7

________ + ________ = ________

Is the number sentence true or false? Circle the correct answer.

17. $8 = 0$ true   false

18. $4 = 5$ true   false

19. $2 + 2 = 4$ true   false

20. $8 - 3 = 5$ true   false

21. $3 + 3 = 6$ true   false

22. $3 + 7 = 9$ true   false

23. $2 + 5 = 5 + 2$ true   false

24. $3 + 4 = 4 + 5$ true   false

Find a way to make the number sentence true.

Example

4 + 5 = 10 is false.

5 + 5 = 10

4 + 6 = 10

4 + 5 = 9

I can change 4 to 5, or 5 to 6.
I can also change 10 to 9.

25.   9 – 3 = 4

26.   2 + 5 = 8

CHAPTER 5 Shapes and Patterns

Worksheet 1   Exploring Plane Shapes

Match.

1.

 ●   ● triangle

 ●   ● square

 ●   ● circle

 ●   ● rectangle

Color the shapes.

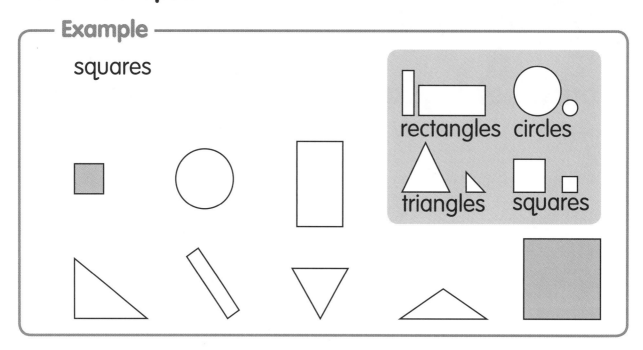

Example

squares

rectangles circles

triangles squares

2. circles

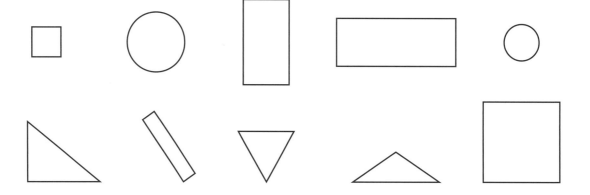

3. triangles

   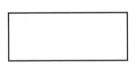

4. rectangles

Trace the sides of the shapes.
Then count the number of sides.

5.  _____

This is a **side** of a triangle.

 side

A triangle has 3 sides.

6. 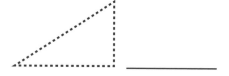 _____   **7.**  _____

Circle the corners of the shapes.
Then count the number of corners.

8.  _____

This is a **corner** of a triangle.

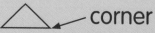 corner

A corner is where two sides meet.
A triangle has 3 corners.

9.  _____   **10.** _____

Name: _____   Date: _____

● **Color the big shapes.**

11.

Color the small shapes.

12.

Fill in the table.

13. Draw each shape in different sizes.

Shape	Big	Small
△		
○		
▭		
◻		

Color the shapes.

14. shapes with only 3 sides

 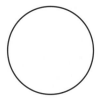

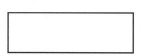

15. shapes with only 4 sides

Color the shapes.

┌─ **Example** ─────────────────────────────────┐

Which shape belongs to Set A?

Set A

└──┘

16. Which shapes belong to Set B?

Set B

 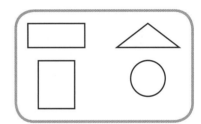

17. Which shapes do <u>not</u> belong to Set C?

Set C

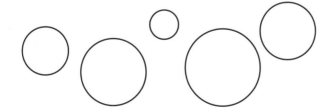 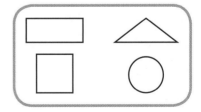

Sort the shapes by <u>size</u>.
Color the shapes that are <u>alike</u>.

18.

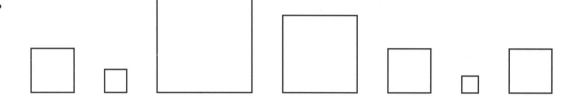

Sort the shapes by <u>shape</u>.
Color the shapes that are <u>alike</u>.

19.

Sort the shapes by the number of <u>corners</u>.
Color the shape that is <u>different</u>.

20.

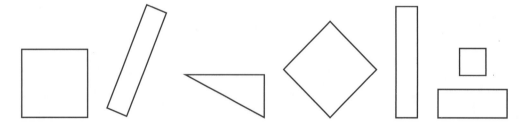

Worksheet 2 Exploring Plane Shapes

Read.
Then answer the questions.

1. Emily has a square piece of paper.
    She folds it and unfolds it.
    Then she draws a line along the fold.
    Now she has two new shapes, A and B.

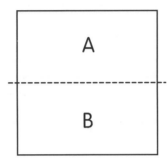

Write *yes* or *no*.

  a. Are Shape A and Shape B the same shape? _____

  b. Are Shape A and Shape B the same size? _____

Count.

  c. How many sides are there?

      Shape A _____   Shape B _____

  d. How many corners are there?

      Shape A _____   Shape B _____

Write *yes* or *no*.

    e. Are Shape A and Shape B <u>alike</u>? _____

Emily then cuts out Shape A and Shape B.

A

B

    f. Can Shape A fit exactly over Shape B? _____

Are the shapes the <u>same</u> shape and size?
Write *yes* or *no*.

2.

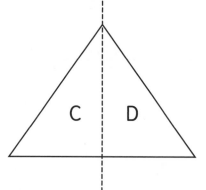

                          Shapes C and D _____

3.

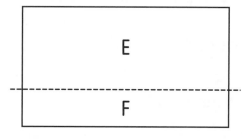

                          Shapes E and F _____

Is the shape cut into halves?
Write *yes* or *no*.

4.

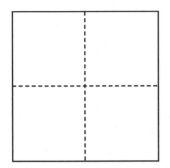

_____

5.

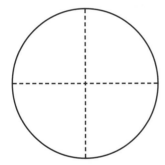

_____

6.

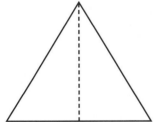

_____

Divide the shape into quarters.
Color one fourth of the shape.

7.

8.

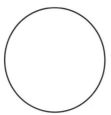

9.

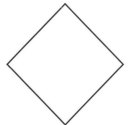

Divide the fruit tart into halves.

10.

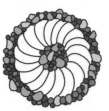

Divide the fruit tart into quarters.

11.

Worksheet 3 Exploring Solid Shapes
Match.

1. sphere   •   •

cylinder   •   •

cube   •   •

pyramid   •   •

cone   •   •

rectangular •   •
prism

Answer the questions.
Circle the shapes.

2. Which shapes are <u>not</u> spheres?

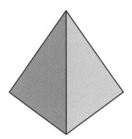

3. Which shapes are <u>not</u> cubes?

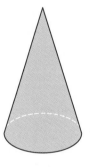

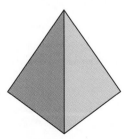

● **Answer the questions.**
Circle the shapes.

4. Which shapes can you stack?

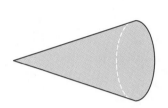

5. Which shapes can you slide?

  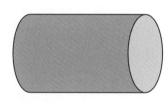

6. Which shapes can you roll?

 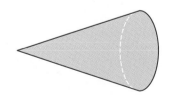 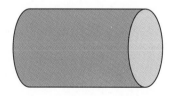

Answer the questions.
Circle the shapes.

7.   Which shape can you stack, slide, and roll?

 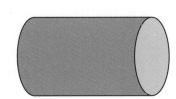

8.   Which shape can you <u>only</u> roll?

 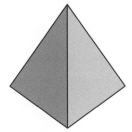

Worksheet 4   Making Pictures and Models with Shapes

Trace the dots.
Name the shapes in the pictures.
Circle the correct names.

┌─ **Example** ───┐

circle (rectangle) (triangle) square

└───┘

1.

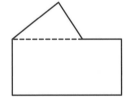

circle   rectangle   triangle   square

2.

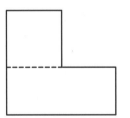

circle   rectangle   triangle   square

3.

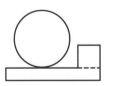

circle   rectangle   triangle   square

4.

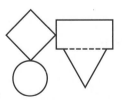

circle   rectangle   triangle   square

Draw a picture with these shapes.

5.

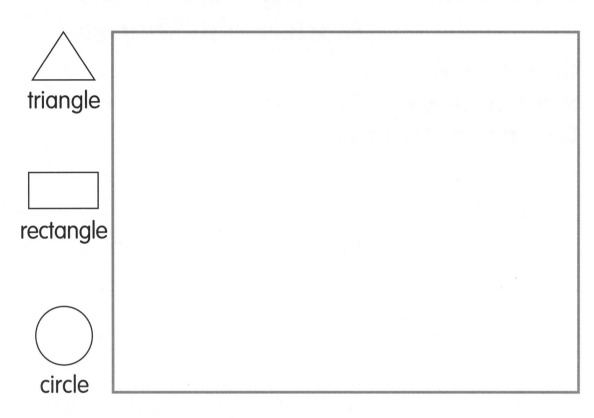

triangle

rectangle

circle

Count the shapes in the picture.
Write the number.

6.

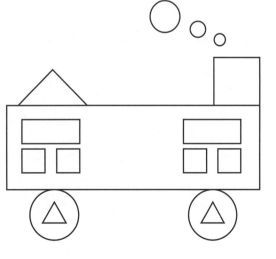

□ square _____

△ triangle _____

○ circle _____

▭ rectangle _____

Worksheet 5   Making Pictures and Models with Shapes

Count the solid shapes in the picture.
Write the number.

1.

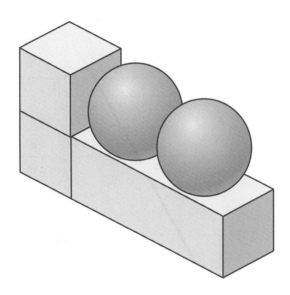

Shape	Number
⬤ sphere	
▮ cylinder	
▮ rectangular prism	
◻ cube	

Count the solid shapes in the picture.
Write the number.

2.

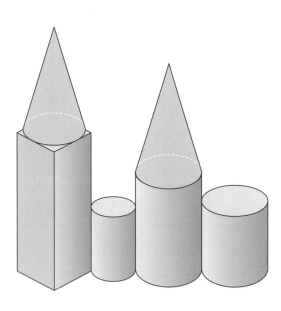

Shape	Number
sphere	
cylinder	
rectangular prism	
pyramid	
cone	

Worksheet 6   Seeing Shapes Around Us

Look at the pictures.
Circle the correct things.

1.   the thing that has the shape of a rectangle

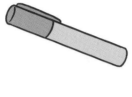
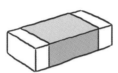

2.   the thing that has the shape of a square

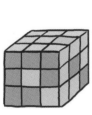

Look at the pictures.
What shapes do you see?
Circle the answers.

3.

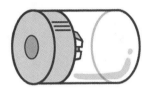

triangle   rectangle

sphere   pyramid

cylinder   cone

4.

circle   square

triangle   cone

cylinder   rectangular prism

Worksheet 7   Making Patterns with Plane Shapes

Complete the patterns.
Circle the missing shape.

Example

This **repeating pattern** changes in **shape.**

triangle, square, triangle, square, triangle, square…

1.

2.

3.

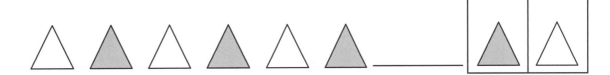

Complete the patterns.
Circle the missing shape.

4.

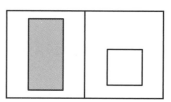

5.

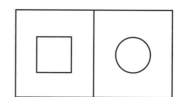

6.

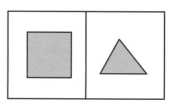

7.

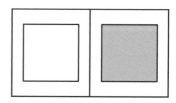

Worksheet 8   Making Patterns with Solid Shapes

Complete the patterns.
Circle the missing shape.

1.

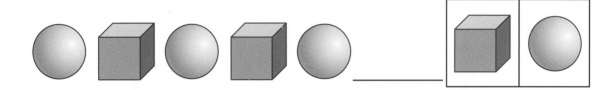

2.

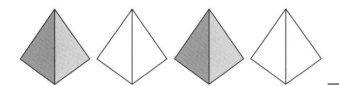 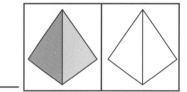

3.

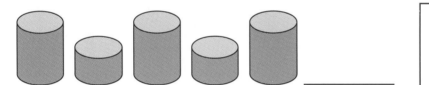 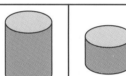

4.

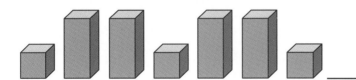 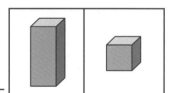

5.

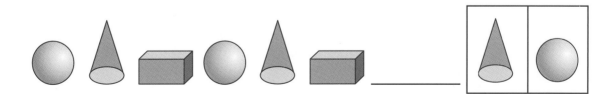

6.

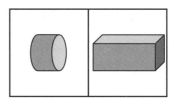

7.

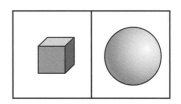

8.

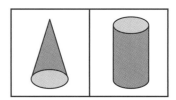

Ordinal Numbers and Position

Worksheet 1   Ordinal Numbers

Look at the picture.
Then write the correct name.

Example

Paulo   Ethan   Grace

3rd   **2nd**   **1st**

_____Grace_____ is first in line.

1. _____ is second in line.

2. _____ is third in line.

Color.

3. 4 dogs

4. the 4th dog

1st

5. 6 balloons

6. the 6th balloon

3rd

Match.

7.

1st	●		●	eighth
2nd	●		●	first
3rd	●		●	seventh
4th	●		●	third
5th	●		●	tenth
6th	●		●	sixth
7th	●		●	fourth
8th	●		●	second
9th	●		●	ninth
10th	●		●	fifth

Fill in the blanks using these words.

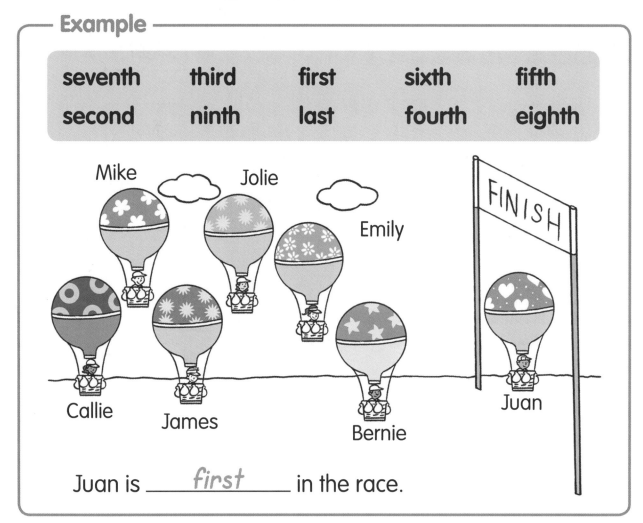

Example

| seventh | third | first | sixth | fifth |
| second | ninth | last | fourth | eighth |

Juan is ___*first*___ in the race.

8. Mike is _____ in the race.

9. Jolie is _____ in the race.

10. James is _____ in the race.

11. Callie is _____ in the race.

She is _____.

Worksheet 2   Position Words

Look at the picture.
Then fill in the blanks.

┌─ **Example** ─────────────────────────────────────┐

Marco   Allen   Benny

| before |
| between |
| after |

Marco is ___*before*___ Allen.

└──┘

1.   Benny is _____ Allen.

2.   Allen is _____ Marco.

3.   Allen is _____ Benny.

4.   Allen is _____ Marco and Benny.

5.   _____ is first in the race.

6.   _____ is last in the race.

Name: _____   Date: _____

**Look at the picture.
Then fill in the blanks.**

Sofia   Gary   Terence   Meredith   Ling

7. _____ is before Meredith.

8. _____ is right after Terence.

9. _____ is just before Terence.

10. Gary is between _____ and _____.

11. Meredith is between _____ and _____.

● **Color.**

┌─ **Example** ─────────────────────────────────┐
the second bee from the left

Left   Right
└──┘

12.   the second bee from the right

Left   Right

13.   the fifth moon from the right

Left   Right

14.   the ninth sticker from the left

Left   Right

Look at the flags.
Then fill in the blanks.

Example

American Canadian Mexican Argentine Brazilian

Left   Right

The Canadian flag is _____*next to*_____ the
American flag.

left
right
next to
last

15. The Argentine flag is fourth from the _____.

16. The Canadian flag is _____ the Mexican flag.

17. The Argentine flag is also _____ the Mexican flag.

18. The American flag is fifth from the _____.

19. The Brazilian flag is _____ from the left.

© Marshall Cavendish International (Singapore) Private Limited.

Worksheet 3   Position Words

Look at the picture.
Then circle the correct word.

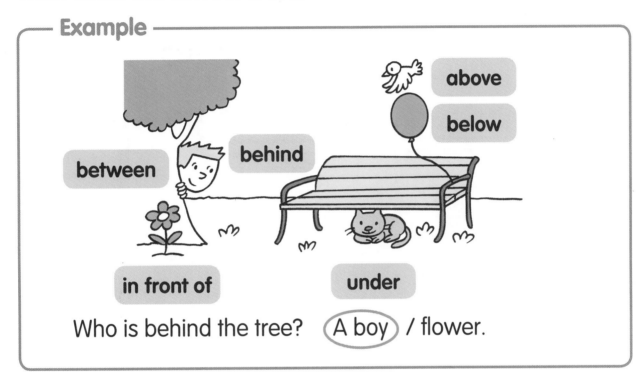

Example

between | behind | above | below | in front of | under

Who is behind the tree?   (A boy) / flower.

1.   What is above the balloon?   A cat / bird.

2.   What is below the bird?   A balloon / flower.

3.   What is under the bench?   A cat / flower.

4.   What is in front of the tree?   A flower / boy.

5.   What is between the boy and the flower?
      A balloon / tree.

Look at the picture.
Then fill in the blanks.

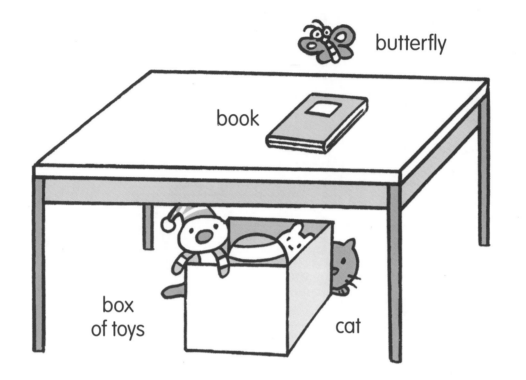

butterfly

book

box
of toys

cat

6. What is above the book?   A _____.

7. What is under the table?   A _____.

8. What is below the butterfly?   A _____.

9. What is behind the box of toys?   A _____.

Look at the picture.
Then fill in the blanks.

up

down

near

far

10. The girl is walking _____ the stairs.

11. The boy is walking _____ the stairs.

12. The boy is _____ the door.

13. The girl is _____ from the door.

Look at the picture.
Then fill in the blanks.

14. The _____ is climbing up the tree.

15. The _____ is under the bench.

16. The _____ is above the boy.

17. The bench is next to the _____.

18. The boy is near the _____.

CHAPTER 7 Numbers to 20

Worksheet 1   Counting to 20

Circle the correct number and word.

1.

4	5	6	7
four	five	six	seven

Match.

2.

5	•	• six •	•	
10	•	• nine •	•	
8	•	• five •	•	
6	•	• eight •	•	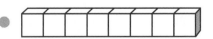
9	•	• two •	•	
2	•	• ten •	•	

Count on.
Fill in the blanks.

Example

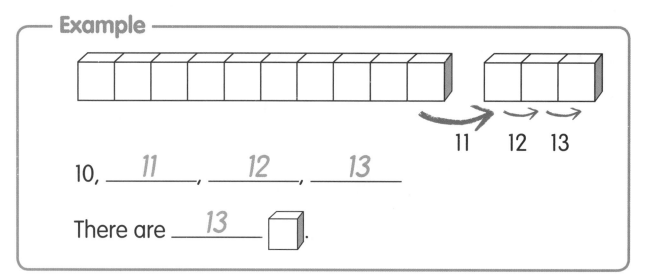

10, __11__, __12__, __13__

There are __13__ ⬜.

3.

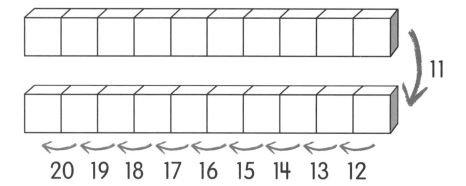

10, _____, _____, _____, _____,

   eleven   twelve   thirteen   fourteen

_____, _____, _____, _____,

   fifteen   sixteen   seventeen   eighteen

_____, _____

   nineteen   twenty

There are _____ ⬜.

Count on.
Fill in the blanks.

4.

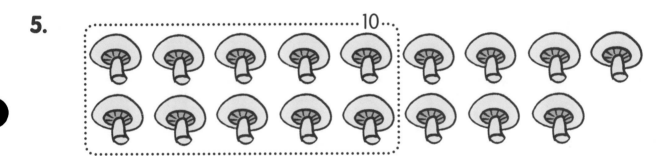

There are _____ penguins.

5.

There are _____ mushrooms.

6.

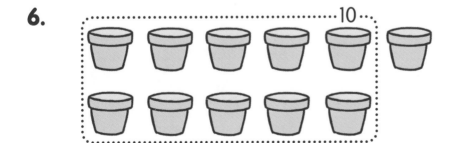

There are _____ pots.

Count.
Fill in the blanks.

7.

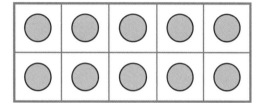 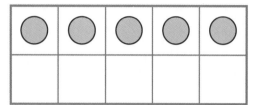

There are _____ .

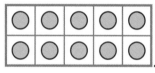 

Count on from

8.

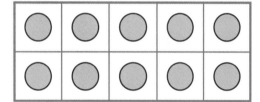 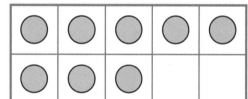

There are _____ ⬤.

Write the numbers.

9. thirteen _____

10. seventeen _____

11. eleven _____

12. twenty _____

13. fourteen _____

14. nineteen _____

15. fifteen _____

16. twelve _____

17. sixteen _____

18. eighteen _____

Match.

19.

11 ●   ● seventeen

20 ●   ● nineteen

15 ●   ● twelve

18 ●   ● sixteen

12 ●   ● twenty

17 ●   ● fourteen

13 ●   ● eleven

19 ●   ● fifteen

14 ●   ● thirteen

16 ●   ● eighteen

Fill in the blanks.

Example

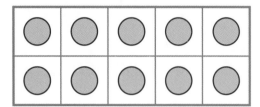
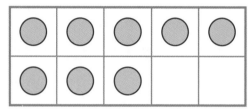

10 and ___8___ make ___18___.

Ten and ___eight___ make eighteen.

___10___ + 8 = ___18___

20.

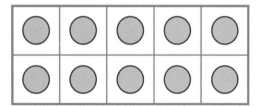
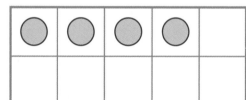

10 and _____ make _____.

Ten and _____ make fourteen.

_____ + 4 = _____

© Marshall Cavendish International (Singapore) Private Limited.

Worksheet 2   Place Value

Circle a group of ten.
Count on.
Then fill in the place-value charts.

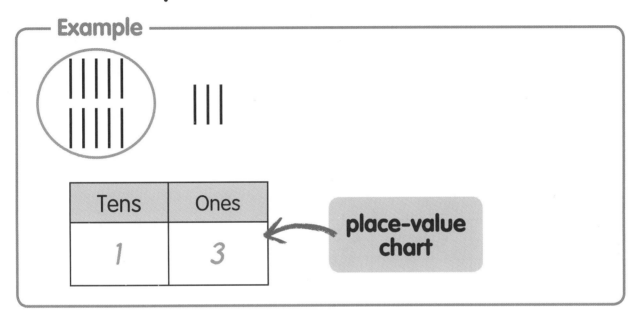

Tens	Ones
1	3

place-value chart

1.

Tens	Ones

2.

Tens	Ones

Fill in the blanks and the place-value charts.

┌─ **Example** ─────────────────────────────────────┐

16 = ____*1*____ ten _____ ones

Tens	Ones
1	

└──┘

3.   13 = _____ ten _____ ones

Tens	Ones

4.   18 = _____ ten _____ ones

Tens	Ones

5.   17 = _____ ten _____ ones

Tens	Ones

Show the number.

Draw ▯ for tens and ☐ for ones.

┌─ **Example** ─────────────────────────────┐

15 = ____1____ ten ____5____ ones

Tens	Ones
▯	☐ ☐ ☐ ☐ ☐

└──┘

6.   19 = _____ ten _____ ones

Tens	Ones

7. 12 = _____ ten _____ ones

Tens	Ones

8. 14 = _____ ten _____ ones

Tens	Ones

Worksheet 3   Comparing Numbers

Compare.
Check (✓) the box that has more items.

1.
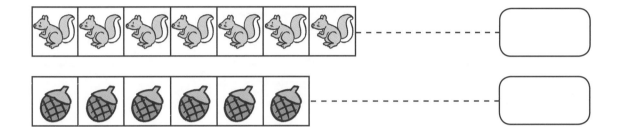

2.
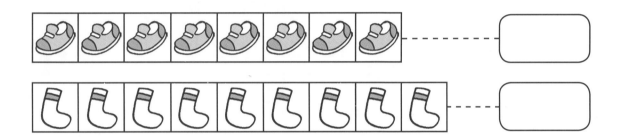

Fill in the blanks.

3.   Write two numbers that are greater than 7.

_____, _____

4.   Write two numbers that are less than 6.

_____, _____

5.   3 more than 8 is _____.

6.   4 less than 9 is _____.

Name: _____ **Date:** _____

Count.
Write the numbers in the boxes.
Then fill in the blanks.

Example

Set A 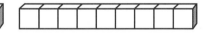 $\boxed{15}$

Set B  $\boxed{12}$

Set A has ____3____ more than Set B.

Set B has ____3____ fewer than Set B.

---

7. Set A  $\boxed{}$

Set B  $\boxed{}$

Set A has _____ more than Set B.

Set B has _____ fewer than Set A.

8. Set A  $\boxed{}$

Set B  $\boxed{}$

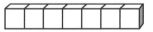

Set A has _____ more than Set B.

Set B has _____ fewer than Set A.

9. Set A  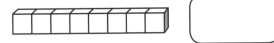 ⬜

Set B 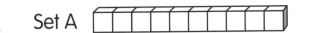  ⬜

Set _____ has _____ more than Set _____.

10. Set A    ⬜

Set B  ⬜

Set _____ has _____ more than Set _____.

11. Set A   ⬜

Set B  ⬜

Set _____ has _____ fewer than Set _____.

Count.
Write the numbers in the boxes.
Then fill in the blanks.

┌─ **Example** ──────────────────────────────────────┐

Set A ▭▭▭▭▭▭▭▭▭▭ ▭▭▭▭▭▭ | 16 |

Set B ▭▭▭▭▭▭▭▭▭▭ ▭▭▭▭ | 14 |

Set A has ____2____ more than Set B.

____16____ is greater than ____14____.

____14____ is less than ____16____.

└──┘

12. Set A ▭▭▭▭▭▭▭▭▭▭ ▭▭▭▭▭▭▭▭▭ | |

Set B ▭▭▭▭▭▭▭▭▭▭ ▭▭▭▭▭ | |

Set A has _____ more than Set B.

_____ is greater than _____.

_____ is less than _____.

13. Set A

Set B

Set A has _____ more than Set B.

_____ is greater than _____.

_____ is less than _____.

14. Set A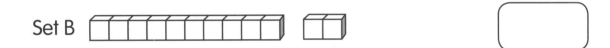

Set B

Set B has _____ fewer than Set A.

_____ is greater than _____.

_____ is less than _____.

15. Set A

Set B

Set A has _____ fewer than Set B.

_____ is greater than _____.

_____ is less than _____.

Complete the place-value charts.
Compare.
Then fill in the blanks.

16.

Tens	Ones
1	6
☐	☐☐☐☐☐ ☐

Tens	Ones
☐	☐☐☐☐☐ ☐☐☐☐

_____ is greater than _____.

_____ is less than _____.

17.

Tens	Ones
☐	☐☐☐☐

Tens	Ones
☐	☐☐☐☐☐ ☐☐☐

_____ is greater than _____.

_____ is less than _____.

Compare.
Use place value to help you.
Write the number that is less in the box.

18.   20   or   10   ⬭

19.   20   or   19   ⬭

Write the number that is greater in the box.

20.   20   or   17   ⬭

21.   20   or   13   ⬭

Write the number that is less in the box.

22.   19   or   11   ⬭

23.   13   or   18   ⬭

Write the number that is greater in the box.

24.   14   or   13   ⬭

25.   16   or   11   ⬭

Name: _____ **Date:** _____

Compare the numbers.
Use place value to help you.
Fill in the blanks.

Example

Compare 20, 14, and 18.

Tens	Ones
2	0

Tens	Ones
1	4

Tens	Ones
1	8

___20___ is the **greatest** number.

___14___ is the **least** number.

---

26. Compare 13, 20, and 19.

_____ is the greatest number.

_____ is the least number.

27. Compare 16, 18, and 13.

_____ is the greatest number.

_____ is the least number.

Worksheet 4 Making Patterns and Ordering Numbers

Complete the number pattern.
Count on.

1.   2, _____, 4, 5, _____, _____, 8

Count back.

2.   _____, 9, 8, _____, _____, 5

Complete the number patterns.

Example

12, 13, ___*14*___, ___*15*___, 16, 17, ___*18*___, ___*19*___

3.   15, _____, _____, _____, 19, 20

4.   19, 18, _____, _____, _____, _____

5.   12, 14, _____, _____, 20

6.   17, _____, 13, 11, _____, _____

The first three ten frames begin a pattern.
Draw  in the ten frames to complete the pattern.

7.

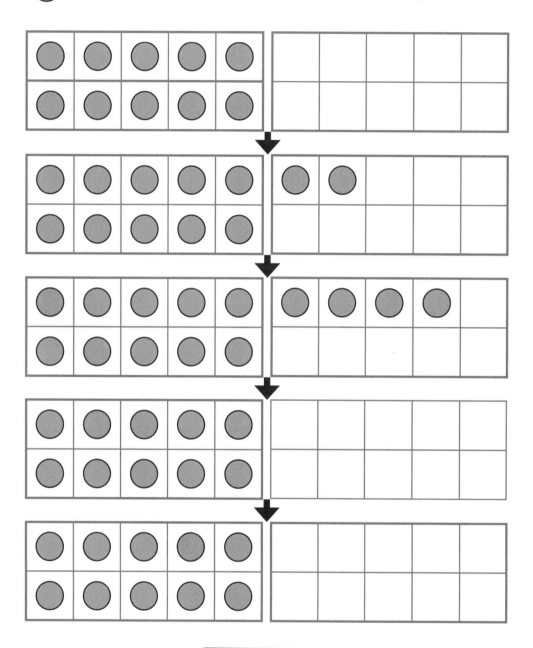

Are we adding more ◯?
How many do we add
each time?

© Marshall Cavendish International (Singapore) Private Limited.

The first three ten frames begin a pattern.
Draw 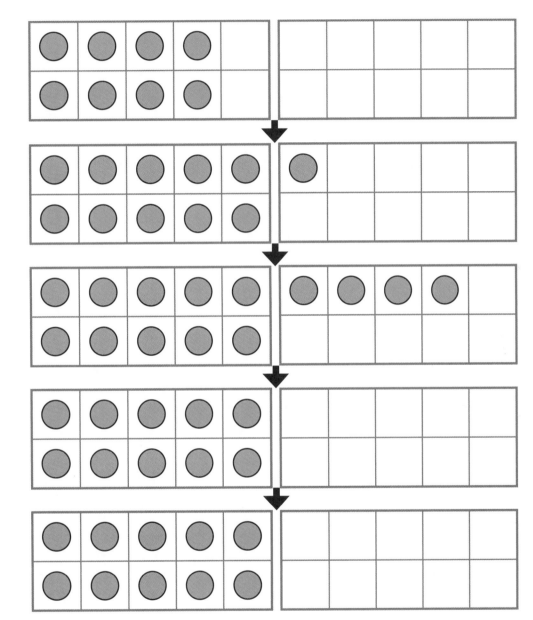 in the ten frames to complete the pattern.

8.

Count on from the greater number.

9. _____ is 1 more than 3.

10. _____ is 2 more than 4.

Count back from the greater number.

11. _____ is 3 less than 8.

12. _____ is 5 less than 10.

13. Draw ☐ to show 3 less than 17.

© Marshall Cavendish International (Singapore) Private Limited.

● **14.** Draw 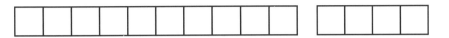 to show 4 more than 14.

● **Order the numbers from greatest to least.**

15. **14**   **16**   **20**

_____, _____, _____
greatest   least

Order the numbers from least to greatest.

16. **15**   **12**   **18**

● _____, _____, _____
least   greatest

Count and order the ☐.
Draw them in the box to make a pattern.

17.

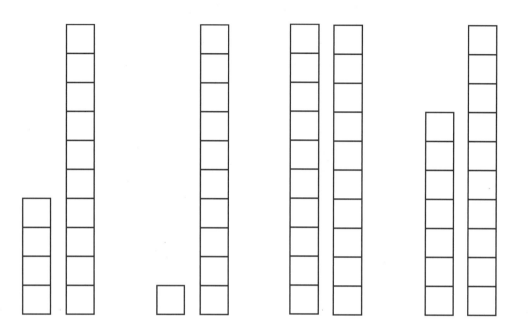

Addition and Subtraction Facts to 20

CHAPTER 8

Worksheet 1   Ways to Add

Write a fact family.

1.

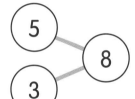

_____ + _____ = _____

_____ + _____ = _____

_____ – _____ = _____

_____ – _____ = _____

2.

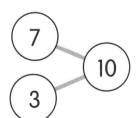

_____ + _____ = _____

_____ + _____ = _____

_____ – _____ = _____

_____ – _____ = _____

Complete the number sentences.

3. 7 + 0 = _____

4. 10 + 0 = _____

5. 8 − 0 = _____

6. 0 − 0 = _____

Fill in the blanks.
Write the related addition facts.

7. ⬤ ⬤ ⬤ ⌀ ⌀ ⌀ ⌀ ⌀

_____ − 5 = 3 ➡ 5 + 3 = _____

8. ⬤ ⬤ ⬤ ⬤ ⬤ ⬤ ⬤ ⬤ ⬤ ⌀ ⌀

_____ − 2 = 9 ➡ _____ + _____ = _____

9. ⬤ ⬤ ⬤ ⬤ ⌀ ⌀

6 − _____ = 4 ➡ 4 + _____ = 6

10. ⬤ ⬤ ⬤ ⬤ ⬤ ⌀ ⌀

7 − _____ = 5 ➡ _____ + _____ = _____

© Marshall Cavendish International (Singapore) Private Limited.

● **Fill in the blanks.**

11.

3 more than 6 is _____.

12.

2 more than 8 is _____.

● **13.**

2 less than 7 is _____.

14.

3 less than 9 is _____.

Complete the number bonds.

15.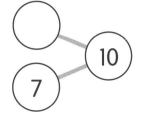

16.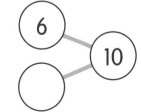

Complete the number bonds.

17.
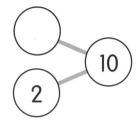

18.
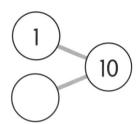

Complete the number sentences.

19. 4 + _____ = 10

20. 7 + _____ = 10

21. _____ + 8 = 10

22. _____ + 1 = 10

Make a 10.
Then add.

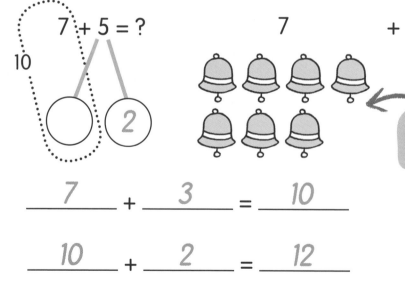

— Example —

7 + 5 = ?

10

2

7 + 5

___7___ + ___3___ = ___10___

___10___ + ___2___ = ___12___

So, ___7___ + ___5___ = ___12___

23.

8   +   3

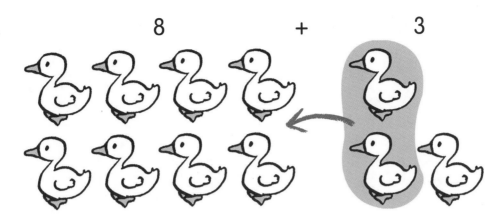

8 + 3 = ?

( )   ( )

_____ + _____ = _____

_____ + _____ = _____

So, _____ + _____ = _____

24.

6   +   7

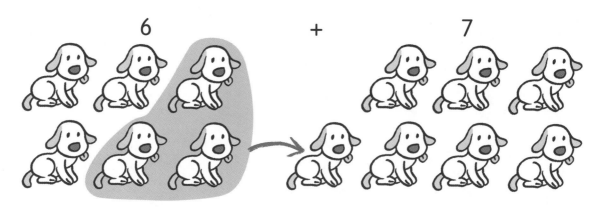

6 + 7 = ?

○   ○

_____ + _____ = _____

_____ + _____ = _____

So, _____ + _____ = _____

Worksheet 2   Ways to Add

Group into a 10 and ones.
Then add.

┌─── Example ──┐

$12 + 6 = ?$

（10）（2）

$\underline{\quad 2 \quad} + \underline{\quad 6 \quad} = \underline{\quad 8 \quad}$

$\underline{\quad 10 \quad} + \underline{\quad 8 \quad} = \underline{\quad 18 \quad}$

So, $\underline{\quad 12 \quad} + \underline{\quad 6 \quad} = \underline{\quad 18 \quad}$

└──┘

1. $7 + 12 = \underline{\hspace{2cm}}$

$\underline{\hspace{2cm}} + \underline{\hspace{2cm}} = \underline{\hspace{2cm}}$

$\underline{\hspace{2cm}} + \underline{\hspace{2cm}} = \underline{\hspace{2cm}}$

So, $\underline{\hspace{2cm}} + \underline{\hspace{2cm}} = \underline{\hspace{2cm}}$

2.   15 + 4 = _____

_____ + _____ = _____

_____ + _____ = _____

So, _____ + _____ = _____

3.   5 + 15 = _____

_____ + _____ = _____

_____ + _____ = _____

So, _____ + _____ = _____

4.   11 + 5 = _____   **5.**   13 + 2 = _____

6.   4 + 15 = _____   **7.**   3 + 16 = _____

Worksheet 3   Ways to Add

Solve.

Example

$2 + 2 =$ ___4___   ← **doubles fact**

◯◯   ◯◯

Double 2 means to add ___2___ more to 2.

---

1. $3 + 3 =$ _____

Double 3 means to add _____ more to 3.

2. $5 + 5 =$ _____

Double 5 means to add _____ more to 5.

The numbers that are added are the **same**.

3. $6 + 6 =$ _____

4. $9 + 9 =$ _____

Solve.
Use doubles plus one facts.

┌─ **Example** ───┐

2 + 3   = 2 + __2__ + __1__

2   1   = __4__ + 1

                         = __5__

┌─────────────────────┐
│ 2 + 3 is a   │
│ **doubles plus**   │
│ **one fact.**   │
└─────────────────────┘
└───┘

5.   7 + 8   = 7 + _____ + _____

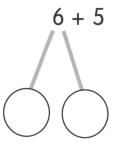   = _____ + 1

                          = _____

6.   6 + 5   = _____ + _____ + 5

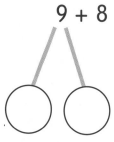   = 1 + _____

                          = _____

7.   9 + 8   = _____ + _____ + 8

                          = 1 + _____

                          = _____

Name: ____________________ Date: ____________

Worksheet 4 Ways to Subtract

Find how many are left.

1.

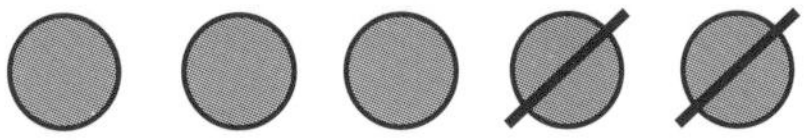

5 – 2 = ________

2.

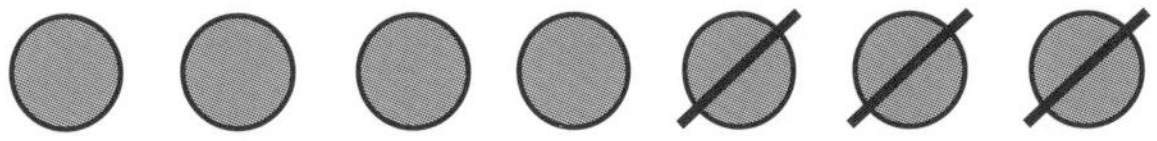

7 – 3 = ________

3.

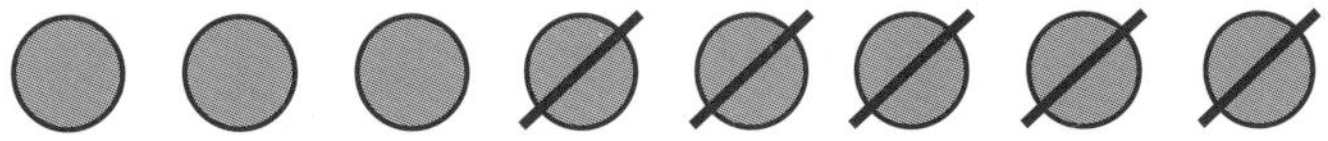

8 – 5 = ________

4.

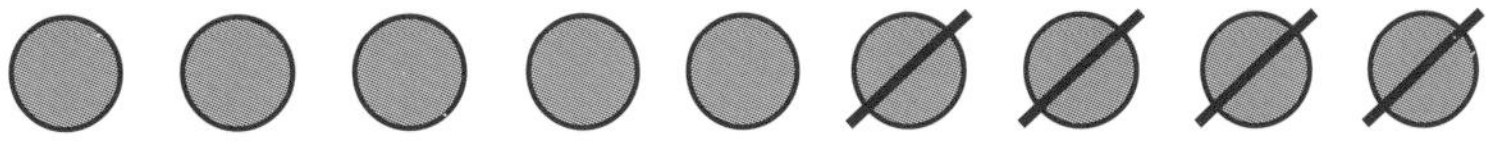

9 – 4 = ________

5.

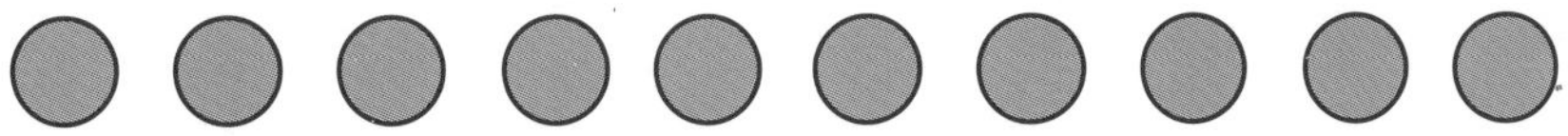

10 – 0 = ________

Name: ______________________ Date: ______________

Group into a 10 and ones.

6.

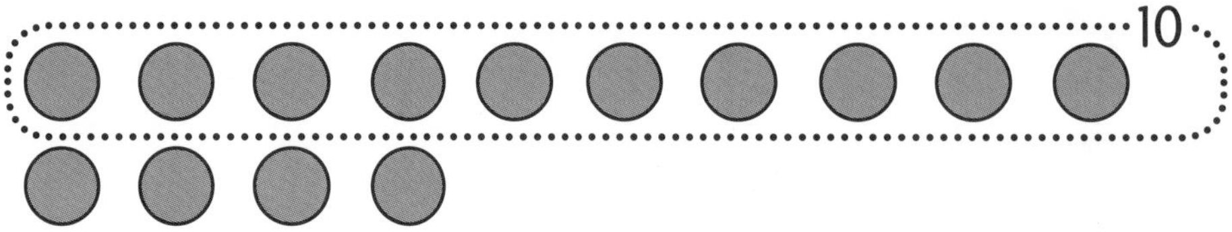

14 = 10 + ________

7.

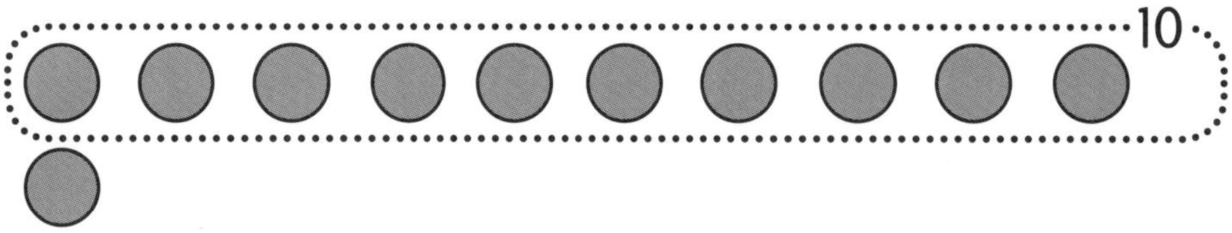

11 = 10 + ________

8.

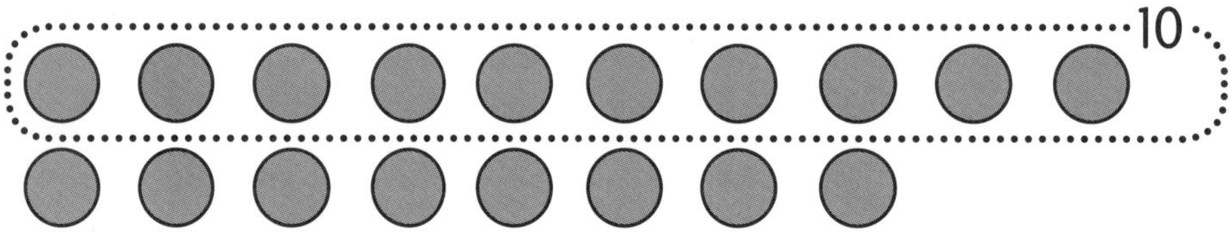

18 = 10 + ________

9.

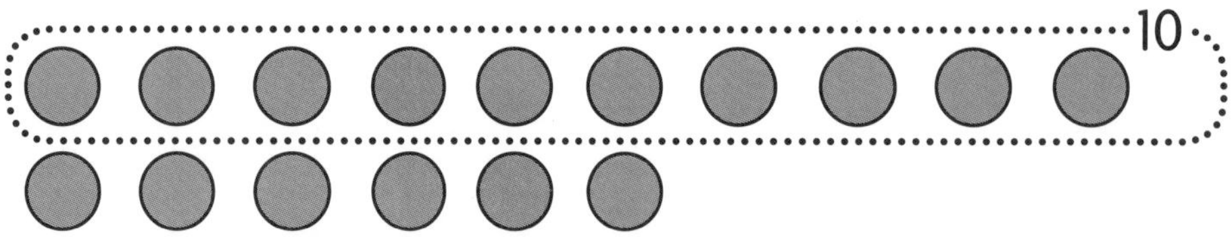

16 = ________ + ________

10.

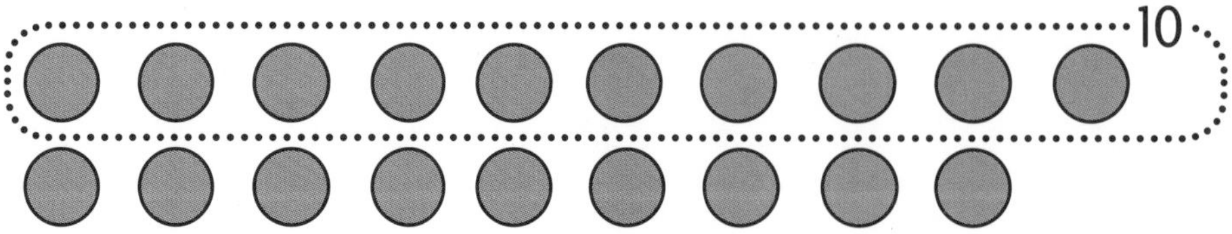

19 = ________ + ________

Group into a 10 and ones.
Then subtract.

─ **Example** ──────────────────────────

17 – 4 = ?

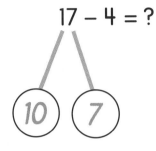

10   7

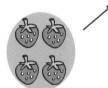

7 – _____4_____ = _____3_____

10 + _____3_____ = _____13_____

So, _____17_____ – _____4_____ = _____13_____

11.   18 – 3 = ?   8 – _____ = _____

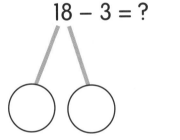

10 + _____ = _____

So, _____ – _____ = _____

12.   16 – 5 = ?   6 – _____ = _____

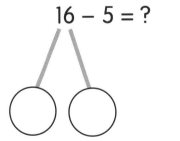

10 + _____ = _____

So, _____ – _____ = _____

13.   19 – 6 = ?   9 – _____ = _____

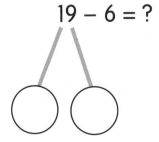

10 + _____ = _____

So, _____ – _____ = _____

Group into a 10 and ones.
Then subtract.

┌─ **Example** ─────────────────────────────────────┐

14 – 7 = ?

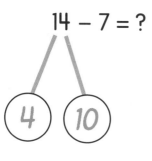

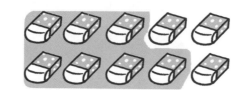

4   10

10 – 7 = ___3___

4 + ___3___ = ___7___

So, 14 – 7 = ___7___

└──┘

14.   12 – 8 = ?   _____ – 8 = _____

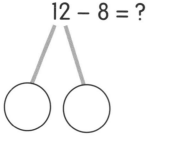

2 + _____ = _____

So, _____ – _____ = _____

15.   13 – 9 = ?   _____ – 9 = _____

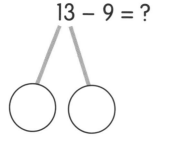

3 + _____ = _____

So, _____ – _____ = _____

16.   11 – 6 = ?   _____ – 6 = _____

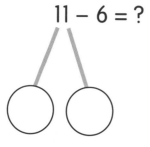

1 + _____ = _____

So, _____ – _____ = _____

17. $12 - 5 =$ _____

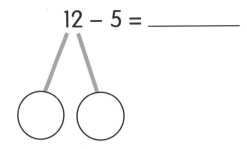

$10 -$ _____ $=$ _____

$2 +$ _____ $=$ _____

18. $13 - 8 =$ _____

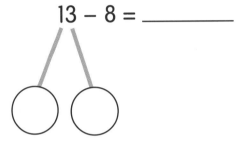

$10 -$ _____ $=$ _____

$3 +$ _____ $=$ _____

19. $14 - 9 =$ _____

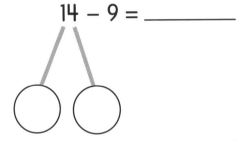

$10 -$ _____ $=$ _____

$4 +$ _____ $=$ _____

20. $15 - 7 =$ _____

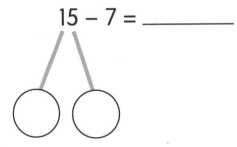

$10 -$ _____ $=$ _____

$5 +$ _____ $=$ _____

Use doubles facts to help you subtract.

Example

Graciela has 4 ribbons.
She gives 2 ribbons to her sister.
How many ribbons does Graciela have now?

$4 - 2 = 2$

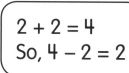

$2 + 2 = 4$
So, $4 - 2 = 2$

Graciela has 2 ribbons now.

21. $6 - 3 =$ _____

22. $8 - 4 =$ _____

23. $18 - 9 =$ _____

24. $14 - 7 =$ _____

25. $20 - 10 =$ _____

Name: _____   **Date:** _____

Worksheet 5   Real-World Problems: Addition and Subtraction Facts

Fill in the blanks.

1.

Ronnie has 9 turtles.
He also has 6 frogs.
How many animals does he have in all?

Ronnie has _____ animals in all.

2.

There were 16 eggs in a basket.
Mr. Thomas took 5 eggs from the basket.
How many eggs are left in the basket?

There are _____ eggs left in the basket.

3.

12 children take part in a swimming race.
5 of the children are girls.
How many boys are in the race?

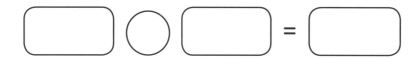

_____ boys are in the race.

4.

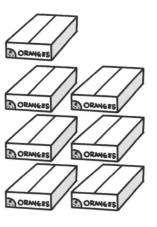 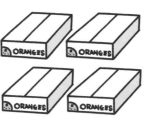

A grocer buys 7 cartons of oranges on Monday.
She buys 4 more cartons on Tuesday.
How many cartons does she buy in all?

She buys _____ cartons in all.

5.

Carlos borrows 4 chapter books.
Lisa borrows 5 chapter books.
How many chapter books do they borrow in all?

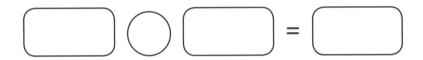

They borrow _____ chapter books in all.

6.

Helena has 5 coins.
Chantel gives her another 8 coins.
How many coins does Helena have now?

Helena has _____ coins now.

7.

17 penguins are in a zoo.
7 penguins are swimming.
How many penguins are <u>not</u> swimming?

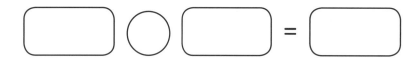

_____ penguins are <u>not</u> swimming.

8.

Rosa invites 13 friends to her party.
7 of her friends are boys.
How many girls are at the party?

_____ girls are at the party.

 **Length**

Worksheet 1   Comparing Two Things

Count.

1.

There are _____ in all.

2.

There are _____ in all.

Compare these numbers.

9   5   18

3.   Which is the greatest? _____

4.   Which is the least? _____

Look at the picture.
Then fill in the blanks using the words.

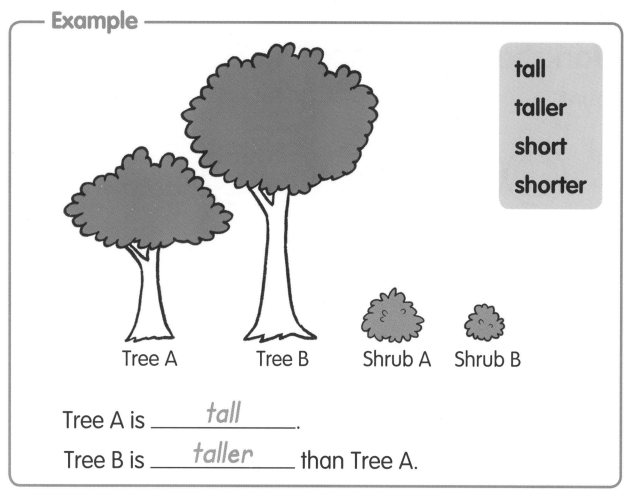

── Example ──────────────────────────

Tree A   Tree B   Shrub A   Shrub B

tall
taller
short
shorter

Tree A is _____*tall*_____ .

Tree B is _____*taller*_____ than Tree A.

5.   Shrub A is _____.

6.   Shrub B is _____ than Shrub A.

● **Circle the correct answer.**

7.   Who is taller?

● **8.**   Which is shorter?

Look at the picture.
Then fill in the blanks using the words.

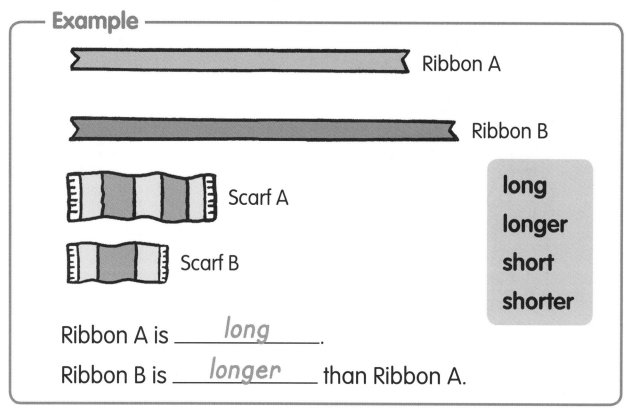

— Example —

Ribbon A

Ribbon B

Scarf A

Scarf B

long
longer
short
shorter

Ribbon A is _____*long*_____.
Ribbon B is _____*longer*_____ than Ribbon A.

9. Scarf A is _____.

10. Scarf B is _____ than Scarf A.

●

Circle the correct answer.

11. Which is longer?

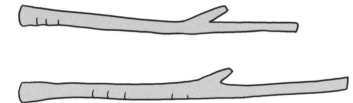

12. Which is shorter?

●

13. Which is longer?

●

Draw.

14. a taller tree

15. a longer string

Fill in the blanks.

16. Which is taller?
Which is shorter?

The tree is _____ than the shrub.

The shrub is _____ than the tree.

17. Which is shorter?
Which is longer?

The truck is _____ than the train.

The train is _____ than the truck.

Fill in the blanks with the words.

| taller   shorter   longer |

18. The table is _____ than the stool.

19. The stool is _____ than the table.

20. The pencil is _____ than the ruler.

21. The ruler is _____ than the pencil.

22. The cat is _____ than the dog.

23. The dog is _____ than the cat.

Worksheet 2   Comparing More Than Two Things

Look at the picture.
Fill in the blanks.

┌─ **Example** ─────────────────────────────┐

Snowy   Patch   Blackie

____*Snowy*____ is taller than Patch.

Patch is taller than ____*Blackie*____.

So, Snowy is taller than ____*Blackie*____.

└──┘

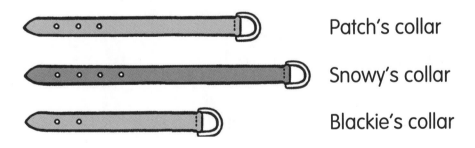

Patch's collar

Snowy's collar

Blackie's collar

1. _____'s collar is longer than Patch's collar.

2. Patch's collar is longer than _____'s collar.

3. So, Snowy's collar is longer than _____'s collar.

 Patch's leash

 Snowy's leash

 Blackie's leash

4. _____'s leash is longer than Patch's leash.

5. Patch's leash is longer than _____'s leash.

6. So, Snowy's leash is longer than _____'s leash.

Patch's kennel   Blackie's kennel   Snowy's kennel

7. _____'s kennel is taller than Patch's kennel.

8. Patch's kennel is taller than _____'s kennel.

9. So, Snowy's kennel is taller than _____'s kennel.

Fill in the blanks with *shortest* or *longest*.

— **Example** —

⬜ eraser

stapler

ruler

The eraser is the ___*shortest*___.
The ruler is the ___*longest*___.

Fill in the blanks with *shortest* or *tallest*.

Eddie   Jenny   Carlo

10.   Carlo is the _____.

11.   Jenny is the _____.

Fill in the blanks with *shortest* or *longest*.

pencil case

paper clip

ruler

12. The pencil case is the _____.

13. The paper clip is the _____.

Fill in the blanks with *shortest* or *tallest*.

giraffe

zebra

elephant

14. The giraffe is the _____.

15. The zebra is the _____.

Name: ____________________ Date: ____________

16. Draw a line.
Make it the shortest line.

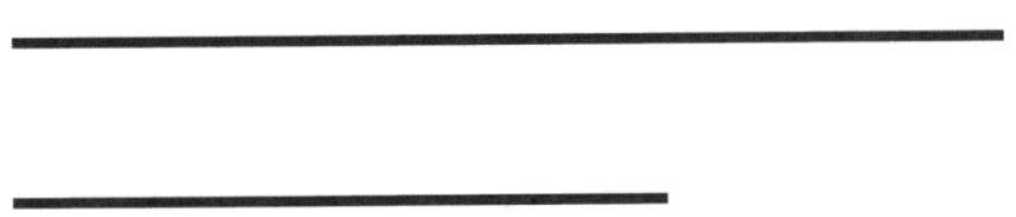

17. Draw a building.
Make it the tallest building.

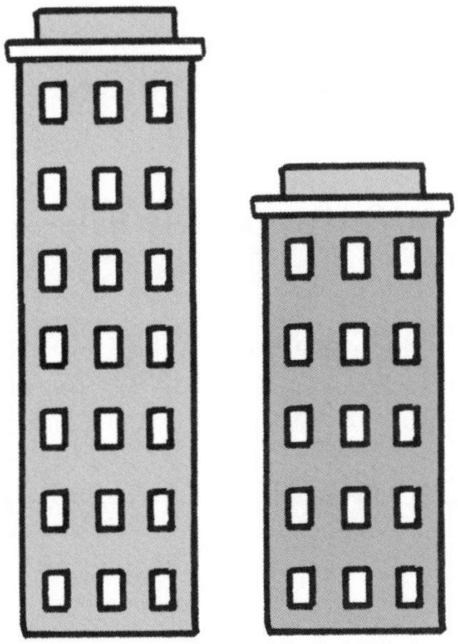

Fill in the blanks with *taller, tallest, shorter,* or *shortest*.

18. The horse is _____ than the monkey.

19. The horse is _____ than the elephant.

20. The elephant is _____ than the monkey.

21. The monkey is _____ than the elephant.

22. The elephant is the _____ animal.

23. The monkey is the _____ animal.

Worksheet 3 Using a Start Line

Fill in the blanks.

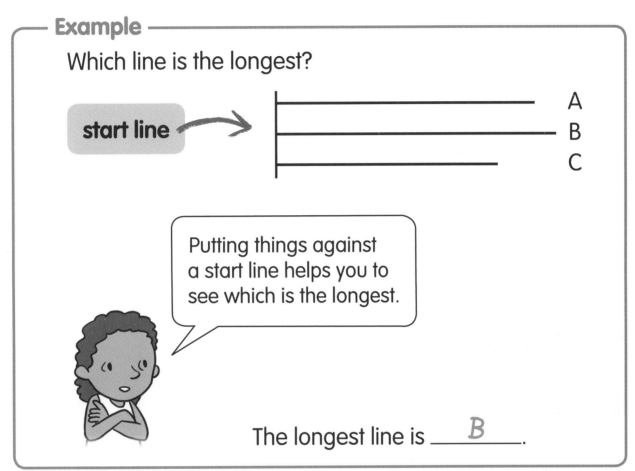

--- Example ---

Which line is the longest?

start line →

A
B
C

Putting things against a start line helps you to see which is the longest.

The longest line is ___B___.

1.   The shortest line is _____.

Cut out the strips of paper.
Paste them along the start line.
Then answer the questions.

Start
Line

2. Which strip is the longest? _____

3. Which strip is the shortest? _____

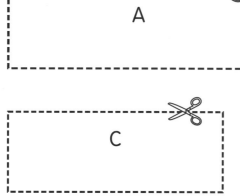

A

C

B

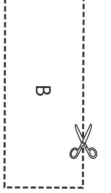

Worksheet 4   Measuring Things

Count.
Write the number in the boxes.

1.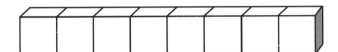

2.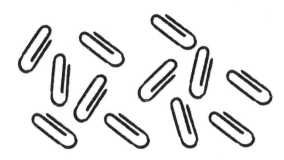

Fill in the blanks with *greater* or *less*.

3.   8 is _____ than 3.

4.   6 is _____ than 9.

Fill in the blanks.

5.   _____, _____, and _____ are numbers
     that are less than 10.

6.   _____, _____, _____, and _____ are
     numbers that are less than 20.

Look at the numbers.
Fill in the blanks with *greatest* or *least*.

4   8   2

7.   8 is the _____ number.

8.   2 is the _____ number.

Count.
Fill in the blanks.

9.

The comb is about _____  long.

10.

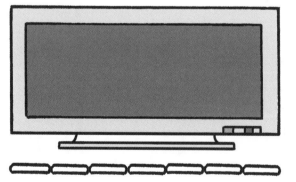

The television set is about _____ long.

11.

The box of crackers is about _____  long.

12.

The book is about _____  long.

13.

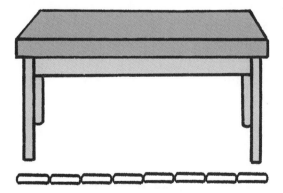

The table is about _____ ⬭ long.

Fill in the blanks.
What is the length of each tape?

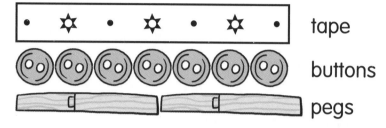

tape

buttons

pegs

The tape is about ___7___ buttons long.

It is about ___2___ pegs long.

14.

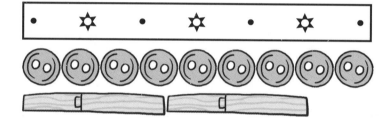

The tape is about _____ buttons long.

It is about _____ pegs long.

15.

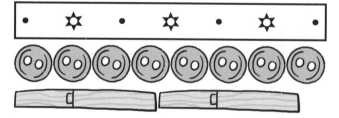

The tape is about _____ buttons long.

It is about _____ pegs long.

Worksheet 5   Finding Length in Units

Count.
Fill in the blanks.

1 ⊂⊃ stands for 1 unit.

┌─ **Example** ────────────────────────┐

The collar is about ___*8*___ units long.

└──────────────────────────────────────┘

1.

The toy bus is about _____ units long.

2.

The card is about _____ units long.

3. 1  stands for 1 unit.

The umbrella is about _____ units long.

4. 1 ⬜ stands for 1 unit.

The toy train is about _____ units long.

5. 1 ⚾ stands for 1 unit.

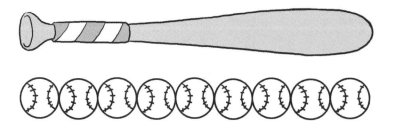

The baseball bat is about _____ units long.

● **Look at the picture.**
Fill in the blanks.

1 ⬭ stands for 1 unit.

Example

The rope is about ___17___ units long.

___17___ is 10 and ___7___.

●

Ribbon A   Ribbon B

6.   Ribbon A is about _____ units long.

7.   Ribbon B is about _____ units long.

_____ is 10 and _____.

8.   Ribbon _____ is longer than Ribbon _____.

Look at the picture.
Fill in the blanks.

1 ☐ stands for 1 unit. Use the words in the box to help you.

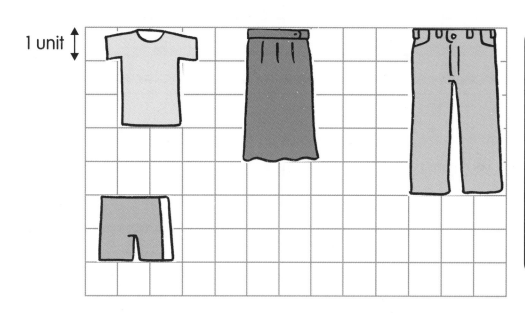

1 unit ↕

short
shorter
shortest
long
longer
longest

9. The T-shirt is _____ units long.

10. The shorts are _____ units long.

11. The pants are _____ units long.

12. The skirt is _____ units long.

13. The T-shirt is _____ than the skirt.

14. The pants are _____ than the skirt.

15. The pants are the _____ item of clothing.

16. The shorts are the _____ item of clothing.

Answers

Chapter 1

Worksheet 1

1.

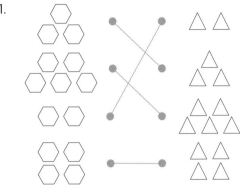

2. 3   3. 8   4. 6
5. 3   6. 1; 4; 6; 2   7. 8

8.

9.

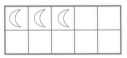

10.

11.

12.

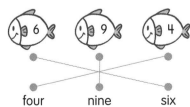

four   nine   six

13.

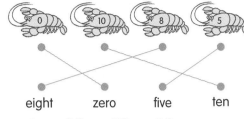

eight   zero   five   ten

14.

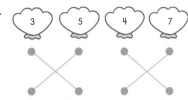

five   three   seven   four

15. seven   16. nine   17. three
18. six   19. ten

Worksheet 2

1. fewer   2. same
3. more   4. fewer, more
5. more, fewer

6.

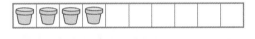

7.

8.

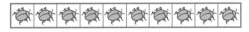

9.

10. 7; 9   11. 8; 4   12. 6; 5
13. ducks; goats (Accept goats; ducks)

14. 8
   (Other possible answers: 9, 10)
15. 1
   (Other possible answers: 0, 2, 3)

Worksheet 3

1. 1, 2, <u>3</u>, <u>4</u>, 5
2. <u>1</u>, 2, <u>3</u>, 4, 5
3. 6, 7, <u>8</u>, <u>9</u>, 10
4. <u>6</u>, 7, <u>8</u>, 9, 10
5. <u>6</u>, 7, 8, <u>9</u>, <u>10</u>
6.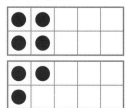
7.
8.
9. 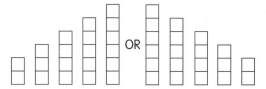 OR

Chapter 2

Worksheet 1

1. 3   2. 2   3. 3; 5
4.
5.
6.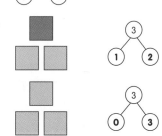

7.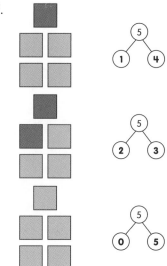

Worksheet 2

1.
2.
3.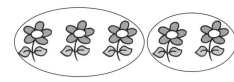

4. 2; 4; 6   5. 1; 6; 7   6. 4; 5; 9

Worksheet 3

1.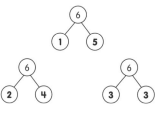
2.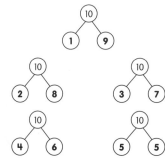

© Marshall Cavendish International (Singapore) Private Limited.

Chapter 3

Worksheet 1

1. 4
2. 7
3. 1, 2, 3, 4, <u>5</u>, <u>6</u>
4. 6, 7, 8, <u>9</u>, <u>10</u>
5. 6, <u>7</u>, 8, <u>9</u>, <u>10</u>
   6 + 4 = <u>10</u>
6. <u>4</u>, <u>5</u>, <u>6</u>
   4 + 2 = <u>6</u>
7. <u>5</u>, <u>6</u>, <u>7</u>, <u>8</u>
   5 + 3 = <u>8</u>
8. <u>3</u> is added on to <u>7</u>.
   7, <u>8</u>, <u>9</u>, <u>10</u>
   <u>10</u> is 3 more than 7.
9. 6, <u>7</u>, <u>8</u>, <u>9</u>, <u>10</u>
   <u>10</u> is 4 more than 6.
10. 8; 8
11. 9; 9
12. 8; 8
13. 10; 10
14. 8
15. 10
16. 1
17. 7

Worksheet 2

1.
2. 2 + 4 = 6
3. 5 + 2 = 7
4. 3 + 7 = 10

5. 3 + 4 = 7
6. 7 + 2 = 9
7.
   5 + 4 = 9   4 + 5 = 9
8. Answers vary.

Worksheet 3

1. <u>6</u> crayons are in the box.
   <u>4</u> crayons are outside the box.
   <u>6</u> + <u>4</u> = 10
   There are <u>10</u> crayons in all.

2. There are <u>2</u> white birds.
   There are <u>7</u> gray birds.
   2 + 7 = 9
   There are <u>9</u> birds in all.

3. Alice has <u>2</u> white cats.
   She has <u>5</u> spotted cats.
   2 + 5 = 7
   Alice has <u>7</u> cats in all.

4. Janice buys <u>3</u> grapefruits.
   Penny buys <u>6</u> grapefruits.
   3 + 6 = 9
   Janice and Penny buy <u>9</u> grapefruits in all.

5. José has <u>8</u> white balls.
   He also has <u>2</u> black balls.
   8 + 2 = 10
   José has <u>10</u> balls in all.

6. Mary has <u>0</u> muffins on Plate A.
   She has <u>7</u> muffins on Plate B.
   0 + 7 = 7
   Mary has <u>7</u> muffins in all.

7. Terence has <u>3</u> toy cars.
   He has <u>5</u> toy trains.
   3 + 5 = 8
   Terence has <u>8</u> toys in all.

Worksheet 4

1. 5 + 3 = 8; 8

2. 3 + 6 = 9; 9

3. 7 + 2 = 9; 9

4. 9 + 0 = 9; 9

Chapter 4

Worksheet 1

1. 4, 5, <u>6</u>, <u>7</u>, 8   2. 3, 4, <u>5</u>, <u>6</u>, <u>7</u>, 8

3. 8, 7, <u>6</u>, <u>5</u>, <u>4</u>   4. 5, 4, <u>3</u>, 2, <u>1</u>, <u>0</u>

5. 7   6. 8

7.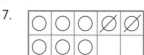
   8 – 2 = <u>6</u>

8.
   9 – 5 = <u>4</u>

9. 7 – <u>3</u> = <u>4</u>   10. 9 – <u>4</u> = <u>5</u>

11. 6 – <u>2</u> = <u>4</u>   12. 8 – <u>3</u> = <u>5</u>

13.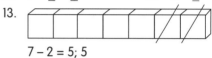
   7 – 2 = <u>5</u>; 5

14.
   8 – <u>3</u> = <u>5</u>; 5

15.
   10 – <u>6</u> = <u>4</u> ; 4

16. 3; 3   17. 4; 4
18. 5; 5   19. 5; 5
20. 3; 3   21. 2; 6
22. 5; 1   23. 7; 3
24. 0; 4

Worksheet 2

1.

2.
   4 – 1 = <u>3</u>

3.
   9 – 4 = <u>5</u>

4.
   5 – 2 = 3

© Marshall Cavendish International (Singapore) Private Limited.

5.

7 – 5 = 2

6.

10 – 2 = 8

7.

6 – 1 = 5

Worksheet 3

1. 7; 4
   7 – 4 = 3; 3

2. 8; 2
   8 – 2 = 6; 6

3. 5; 3
   5 – 3 = 2; 2

4. 6; 4
   6 – 4 = 2; 2

5. 7; 3
   7 – 3 = 4; 4

Worksheet 4

1. 7 – 3 = 4; 4

2. 8 – 4 = 4; 4

3. 10 – 4 = 6; 6

4. 7 – 2 = 5; 5

Worksheet 5

1. 3 + 7 = 10
   7 + 3 = 10
   10 – 7 = 3
   10 – 3 = 7

2. 5 + 2 = 7
   2 + 5 = 7
   7 – 2 = 5
   7 – 5 = 2

3. 3 + 7 = 10
   7 + 3 = 10
   10 – 7 = 3
   10 – 3 = 7

4. 5 + 3 = 8
   3 + 5 = 8
   8 – 3 = 5
   8 – 5 = 3

5. 2 + 3 = 5
   3 + 2 = 5
   5 – 3 = 2
   5 – 2 = 3

6. 6 + 2 = 8
   2 + 6 = 8
   8 – 2 = 6
   8 – 6 = 2

7. 1,
    3 + 1 = 4
    1 + 3 = 4   OR
    4 − 1 = 3
    4 − 3 = 1

    7,
    3 + 4 = 7
    4 + 3 = 7
    7 − 4 = 3
    7 − 3 = 4

8. 8; 8; 8
9. 4; 4; 4
10. 4 + 5 = 9
    9 − 4 = 5
11. 4 + 2 = 6
    6 − 2 = 4
12. 0 + 3 = 3
    3 − 0 = 3
13. 8 − 5 = 3
    3 + 5 = 8
14. 9 − 2 = 7
    2 + 7 = 9
15. 9 − 4 = 5
    4 + 5 = 9
16. 10 − 3 = 7
    3 + 7 = 10
17. false
18. false
19. true
20. true
21. true
22. false
23. true
24. false
25. 9 − 5 = 4
    7 − 3 = 4
    9 − 3 = 6
26. 3 + 5 = 8
    2 + 6 = 8
    2 + 5 = 7

Chapter 5

Worksheet 1

1.

2.

3.

4.
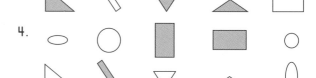

5. 4
6. 3
7. 4
8.
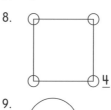   4

9.
   0

10.
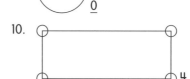   4

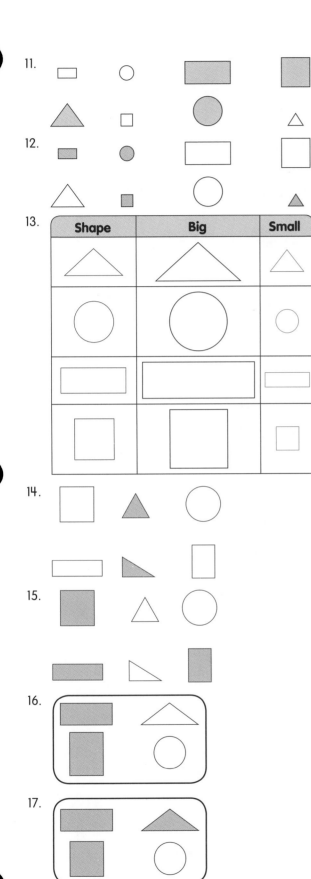

11.

12.

13.

Shape	Big	Small

14.

15.

16.

17.

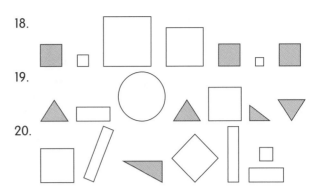

18.

19.

20.

Worksheet 2

1. a. yes
   b. yes
   c. Shape A: 4
      Shape B: 4
   d. Shape A: 4
      Shape B: 4
   e. yes
   f. yes

2. yes

3. no

4. no

5. no

6. yes

7.

8.

9.

10.

11.

Worksheet 3

1.
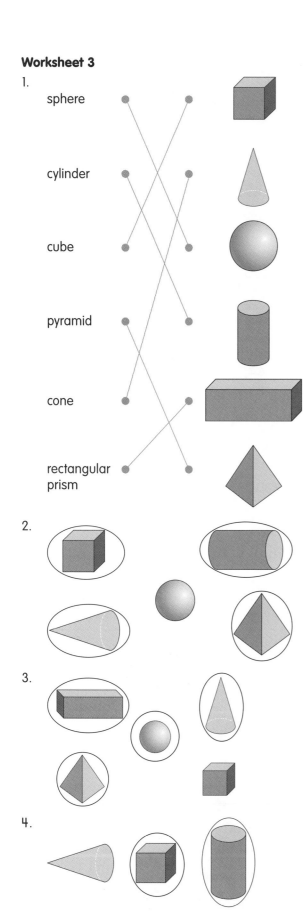

sphere

cylinder

cube

pyramid

cone

rectangular prism

2.

3.

4.

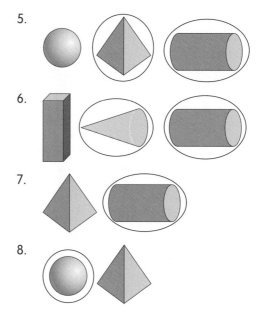

5.

6.

7.

8.

Worksheet 4

1. rectangle, triangle
2. rectangle, square
3. circle, rectangle, square
4. circle, rectangle, triangle, square
5. Answers vary.
6. square: 5
   triangle: 3
   circle: 5
   rectangle: 3

Worksheet 5

1.

Shape		Number
	sphere	2
	cylinder	0
	rectangular prism	1
	cube	2

2.

Shape	Number
sphere	0
cylinder	3
rectangular prism	1
pyramid	0
cone	2

Worksheet 6

1.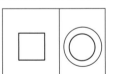

2.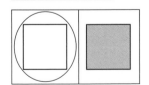

3. cylinder

4. rectangular prism

Worksheet 7

1.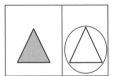

2.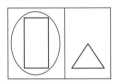

3.

4.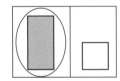

5.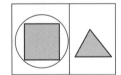

6.

7.

Worksheet 8

1.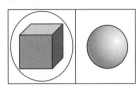

2.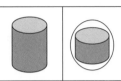

3.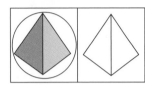

4.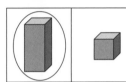

5.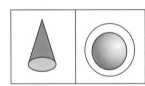

6.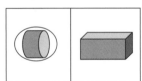

7.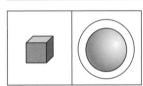

8.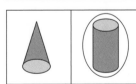

Chapter 6

Worksheet 1

1. Ethan

2. Paulo

3.

4.
                1st

5.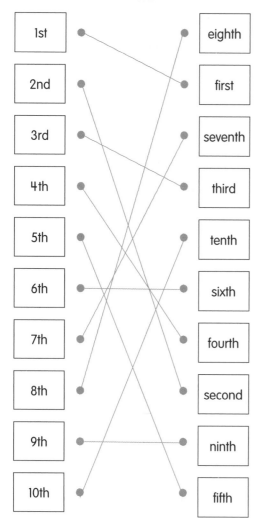

6.

3rd

7.

1st	—	eighth
2nd	—	first
3rd	—	seventh
4th	—	third
5th	—	tenth
6th	—	sixth
7th	—	fourth
8th	—	second
9th	—	ninth
10th	—	fifth

8. sixth
10. fifth

9. fourth
11. seventh; last

Worksheet 2

1. after
3. before
5. Marco
7. Ling
9. Meredith
11. Terence; Ling

2. after
4. between
6. Benny
8. Gary
10. Sofia; Terence

12.

13.

14.

15. left
17. next to
19. fifth or 5th

16. next to
18. right

Worksheet 3

1. A bird
3. A cat
5. A tree
7. box of toys or cat
9. cat
11. down
13. far
15. frog
17. tree

2. A balloon
4. A flower
6. butterfly
8. book
10. up
12. near
14. cat
16. balloon
18. dog

Chapter 7

Worksheet 1

1. 5; five
2.

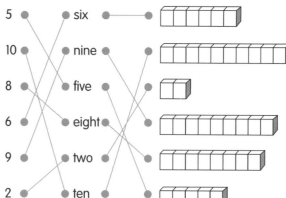

5	six
10	nine
8	five
6	eight
9	two
2	ten

3. 11, 12, 13, 14,
   15, 16, 17, 18,
   19, 20
   There are 20 ☐.

4. 14
7. 15
10. 17
13. 14
16. 12

5. 17
8. 18
11. 11
14. 19
17. 16

6. 11
9. 13
12. 20
15. 15
18. 18

19.

11	seventeen
20	nineteen
15	twelve
18	sixteen
12	twenty
17	fourteen
13	eleven
19	fifteen
14	thirteen
16	eighteen

(lines connecting numbers to words)

20. 10 and 4 make 14.
Ten and four make fourteen.
10 + 4 = 14

Worksheet 2

1.

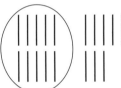

Tens	Ones
1	8

2.

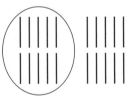

Tens	Ones
1	10

3. 13 = 1 ten 3 ones

Tens	Ones
1	3

4. 18 = 1 ten 8 ones

Tens	Ones
1	8

5. 17 = 1 ten 7 ones

Tens	Ones
1	7

6. 19 = 1 ten 9 ones

Tens	Ones

7. 12 = 1 ten 2 ones

Tens	Ones

8. 14 = 1 ten 4 ones

Tens	Ones

Worksheet 3

1.  ✓

 ◯

2.  ◯

 ✓

3. Any two numbers from 8 onwards,
for example: 9, 10

4. Any two numbers from 1 to 5, for example: 2,4

5. 11   6.   5

7. Set A: 19
Set B: 14
5; 5

8. Set A: 17
   Set B: 13
   4; 4

9. Set A: 18
   Set B: 12
   A; 6; B

10. Set A: 11
    Set B: 15
    B; 4; A

11. Set A: 13
    Set B: 14
    A; 1; B

12. Set A: 20
    Set B: 15
    Set A has 5 more than Set B.
    20 is greater than 15.
    15 is less than 20.

13. Set A: 19
    Set B: 11
    Set A has 8 more than Set B.
    19 is greater than 11.
    11 is less than 19.

14. Set A: 18
    Set B: 12
    Set B has 6 fewer than Set A.
    18 is greater than 12.
    12 is less than 18.

15. Set A: 13
    Set B: 15
    Set A has 2 fewer than Set B.
    15 is greater than 13.
    13 is less than 15.

16. 1; 9
    19 is greater than 16.
    16 is less than 19.

17. 1; 4; 1; 8
    18 is greater than 14.
    14 is less than 18.

18. 10   19. 19   20. 20
21. 20   22. 11   23. 13
24. 14   25. 16   26. 20; 13
27. 18; 13

Worksheet 4

1. 2, <u>3</u>, 4, 5, <u>6</u>, <u>7</u>, 8   2. <u>10</u>, 9, 8, <u>7</u>, <u>6</u>, 5
3. 15, <u>16</u>, <u>17</u>, <u>18</u>, 19, 20   4. 19, 18, <u>17</u>, <u>16</u>, <u>15</u>, <u>14</u>
5. 12, 14, <u>16</u>, <u>18</u>, 20   6. 17, <u>15</u>, 13, 11, <u>9</u>, <u>7</u>

7.
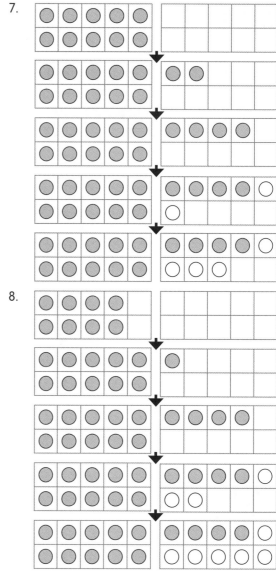

8.

9. 4   10. 6
11. 5   12. 5
13.
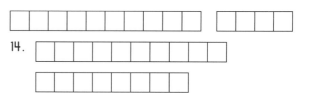

14.

15. 20, 16, 14   16. 12, 15, 18
17. 11, 14, 17, 20
    or
    20, 17, 14, 11

© Marshall Cavendish International (Singapore) Private Limited.

Chapter 8

Worksheet 1

1. $5 + 3 = 8$
   $3 + 5 = 8$
   $8 - 5 = 3$
   $8 - 3 = 5$

2. $7 + 3 = 10$
   $3 + 7 = 10$
   $10 - 7 = 3$
   $10 - 3 = 7$

3. 7   4. 10
5. 8   6. 0

7. $\underline{8} - 5 = 3 \longrightarrow 5 + 3 = \underline{8}$

8. $\underline{11} - 2 = 9 \longrightarrow \underline{2} + \underline{9} = \underline{11}$

9. $6 - \underline{2} = 4 \longrightarrow 4 + \underline{2} = 6$

10. $7 - \underline{2} = 5 \longrightarrow \underline{2} + \underline{5} = \underline{7}$

11. 9   12. 10
13. 5   14. 6

15.   16.
17.   18.

19. 6   20. 3
21. 2   22. 9

23. $8 + 2 = 10$
    $10 + 1 = 11$
    $8 + 3 = 11$

24. $3 + 7 = 10$
    $3 + 10 = 13$
    $6 + 7 = 13$

Worksheet 2

1. $7 + 2 = 9$
   $9 + 10 = 19$
   $7 + 12 = 19$

2. $5 + 4 = 9$
   $10 + 9 = 19$
   $15 + 4 = 19$

3. $5 + 5 = 10$
   $10 + 10 = 20$
   $5 + 15 = 20$

4. 16   5. 15
6. 19   7. 19

Worksheet 3

1. 6; 3
2. 10; 5
3. 12
4. 18
5. $7 + \underline{7} + \underline{1}$
   $= \underline{14} + 1$
   $= \underline{15}$
6. $\underline{1} + \underline{5} + 5$
   $= 1 + \underline{10}$
   $= \underline{11}$
7. $\underline{1} + \underline{8} + 8$
   $= 1 + \underline{16}$
   $= \underline{17}$

Worksheet 4

1. 3   2. 4   3. 3
4. 5   5. 10   6. 4
7. 1   8. 8   9. 10; 6
10. 10; 9

11. $8 - \underline{3} = \underline{5}$
    $10 + \underline{5} = \underline{15}$
    So, $\underline{18} - \underline{3} = \underline{15}$

12. $6 - \underline{5} = \underline{1}$
    $10 + \underline{1} = \underline{11}$
    So, $\underline{16} - \underline{5} = \underline{11}$

13. $9 - \underline{6} = \underline{3}$
    $10 + \underline{3} = \underline{13}$
    So, $\underline{19} - \underline{6} = \underline{13}$

14. $\underline{10} - 8 = \underline{2}$
    $\underline{2} + \underline{2} = \underline{4}$
    So, $\underline{12} - \underline{8} = \underline{4}$

15. $\underline{10} - 9 = \underline{1}$
    $\underline{3} + \underline{1} = \underline{4}$
    So, $\underline{13} - \underline{9} = \underline{4}$

16. $\underline{10} - 6 = \underline{4}$
    $\underline{1} + \underline{4} = \underline{5}$
    So, $\underline{11} - \underline{6} = \underline{5}$

17. $12 - 5 = \underline{7}$ $10 - \underline{5} = \underline{5}$
    (2) (10) $2 + \underline{5} = \underline{7}$

18. $13 - 8 = \underline{5}$ $10 - \underline{8} = \underline{2}$
    (3) (10) $3 + \underline{2} = \underline{5}$

19. $14 - 9 = \underline{5}$

    $10 - \underline{9} = \underline{1}$
    $4 + \underline{1} = \underline{5}$

20. $15 - 7 = \underline{8}$
    $10 - \underline{7} = \underline{3}$
    $5 + \underline{3} = \underline{8}$

21. 3   22. 4
23. 9   24. 7
25. 10

Worksheet 5

1. $9 + 6 = 15$; 15
2. $16 - 5 = 11$; 11
3. $12 - 5 = 7$; 7
4. $7 + 4 = 11$; 11
5. $4 + 5 = 9$; 9
6. $5 + 8 = 13$; 13
7. $17 - 7 = 10$; 10
8. $13 - 7 = 6$; 6

Chapter 9

Worksheet 1

1. 7   2. 5
3. 18   4. 5
5. short   6. shorter
7.

8.

9. short   10. shorter
11.
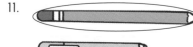

12.
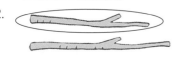

13.

14.

15.

16. taller; shorter
17. shorter; longer
18. taller   19. shorter 20. shorter
21. longer   22. shorter 23. taller

Worksheet 2

1. Snowy   2. Blackie
3. Blackie   4. Snowy
5. Blackie   6. Blackie
7. Snowy   8. Blackie
9. Blackie   10. tallest
11. shortest   12. longest
13. shortest   14. tallest
15. shortest
16. _____

    _____

    _____

17.

18. taller   19. shorter
20. taller   21. shorter
22. tallest   23. shortest

Worksheet 3
1. C   2. A   3. B

Worksheet 4
1. 8   2. 12
3. greater   4. less
5. Accept any three answers from 1 to 9
6. Accept any four answers from 1 to 19
7. greatest
8. least
9. 5   10. 7
11. 6   12. 5
13. 8   14. 9; 2
15. 8; 2

Worksheet 5
1. 4   2. 2
3. 7   4. 6
5. 9   6. 9
7. 12; 12; 2   8. B; A
9. 3   10. 2
11. 5   12. 4
13. shorter   14. longer
15. longest   16. shortest